TRAGEDY: *a view of life*

�֎֎֎

# TRAGEDY: *a view of life*

## BY HENRY ALONZO MYERS

✖✖✖

*Cornell University Press*, ITHACA, NEW YORK

© 1956 by Cornell University

CORNELL  UNIVERSITY  PRESS

LONDON:  GEOFFREY  CUMBERLEGE

OXFORD  UNIVERSITY  PRESS


First published 1956

PRINTED  IN  THE  UNITED  STATES  OF  AMERICA  BY  THE

VAIL-BALLOU  PRESS,  INC.,  BINGHAMTON,  NEW  YORK

✲✲✲

# Preface

DURING his twenty years as teacher of drama and American literature at Cornell University, Henry Alonzo Myers made tragedy a special interest; he wrote and lectured extensively on the subject, exploring its meaning and significance both as a form of art and as a pattern of moral values. Some of his essays and lectures were designed as chapters for a book, *Tragedy: A View of Life*, on which he was working when he died in 1955.

Henry Myers endeavored to answer three questions which he considered basic to the problems of our times: "What is the proper relation of the sciences and arts to one another and to the reality which they seek to describe? Are men equal? Are human fortunes (good and evil) ruled by chance or by fixed conditions which can be

*Preface*

formulated into laws?" In *The Spinoza-Hegel Paradox: A Study of the Choice between Traditional Idealism and Systematic Pluralism,* he made a start on answering the first question. His book, *Are Men Equal? An Inquiry into the Meaning of American Democracy,* is an answer to the second. In *Tragedy: A View of Life,* he desired to define the universal conditions of human values.

I wish to thank Professor Milton R. Konvitz of Cornell University for his devoted, invaluable assistance in organizing the material, Professor John Wendell Dodds of Stanford University and Professor Hubert Crouse Heffner of Indiana University for their most helpful advice and good judgment in matters of form and style, and Professor H. Darkes Albright of Cornell for his expert and informed aid in reading proof.

ELSIE P. MYERS

*Ithaca, New York*
*March, 1956*

✲✲✲

# Contents

*vii*

# Contents

# PART ONE

# Toward a Definition of Tragedy

# I ❋

# The Tragic Attitude

# toward Value

THE philosophy of value, if it is to rise above the level of an academic problem, must bridge the gap which now separates it from its chief source of reliable material, the arts which represent feeling. A union between philosophical method and the arts of personal feeling is clearly needed inasmuch as the philosophy of value is itself a revolt against the philosophical tradition which was content to follow only the needs and problems of the impersonal sciences and which, consequently, found in the uniformity of nature and experience only causal sequence, mechanical determination, and logical or mathematical necessity. Blind to all other forms and patterns of experience, this tradition left values, like opinions, in the philosophical limbo ruled by chance, fortune, or caprice. At best, it taught us, as Spinoza did, to love the cold scientific necessity which rules the world and to repress human values, which have their source in illusion. This love of the universal necessity of the world is an advanced position for the philosopher of science, but it is unnecessarily primitive for the philosopher of value, who is by the nature of his enterprise committed, first, to the principle that values are subject to law, and not to chance, fortune, or caprice, and, secondly, to the principle that bare necessity, order, and law, as revealed by the scientific disciplines, take on a new meaning when revealed in terms of values.

Since inevitability, or orderliness of values, has always been required of tragedy as a representation, and since the very first tragic poet took his problem to be the interpretation in terms of value of the iron bonds of necessity which rule the world, it is evident that the most advanced philosophy of science is pre-Aeschylean in the realm of values, and it is further evident that the philosophy of value must find its material in tragic art, where its axioms are everywhere obeyed, and not in the philosophy of science, where these axioms are avoided on principle. For it is certainly the task of the philosopher to investigate every representation of orderliness in values, and especially to examine those representations which seek to find a law more appropriate to values than the impersonal necessity of the sciences.

## I

What is the tragic attitude toward value, and what is the source of our pleasure in tragedy? The answers to these questions, which seek to get at the nature of a repre-

sentation and the effect of that representation upon a
spectator, must be related as intimately as two points of
view of one and the same thing are related, for both lead
us to the essence of tragedy, to that element constant
in all tragedies which distinguishes the form from other
kinds of representation and expression. This distinct character of tragedy as a form is an empirical fact to be explained by theory rather than a fact established by theory.
We feel this attitude and appreciate it without necessarily
being able to describe it intellectually. Without knowing
the precise chemistry which distinguishes wine from
water, we are nevertheless able to distinguish one from
the other; and in the same way, without knowing the exact
logic which constitutes the tragic attitude toward good
and evil, we are yet able to distinguish tragedy from optimism and pessimism. The tragic attitude is not optimism,
for it does not represent the little that is evil in the world
as rapidly diminishing, and it is not pessimism, for it does
not represent that inevitable obliteration of good which
leads one away from the unyielding persistence of the
tragic hero and toward the resignation and acceptance of
forgetfulness. In like manner tragedy affords its own kind
of pleasure to the spectator. We know by experience
rather than by hypothesis that St. Augustine is wrong in
thinking that the same curiosity, "the lust of the eyes,"
leads us to the theatre and to the scene of sensational or
shocking events. We have seen shocking events, and we
have seen tragedies. They are not the same.

But it is easier to know this than it is to tell how we
know it, for tragedies are, at least when partially considered, spectacles of evil. And it is this partial consideration

which brings about the superficial paradox of tragedy. Tragedy is a spectacle of evil. Evil is precisely that which we do not enjoy. Yet we do enjoy tragedy.

To escape from this superficial paradox it is necessary only to maintain that tragedy is something more than a spectacle of evil, but then it is necessary to explain what the further element is and how it brings us pleasure. Since that further element must be good, it must be one of the three goods here possible. It must be the triumph of good over evil in the action itself; or it must be the triumph of the play as a whole, considered in respect to its diction, melody, and artistic proportion, over the evil in the action proper; or it must be the relation of constant implication between good and evil in the action, a relation which could please us by its suggestion of order and law and by its insistence upon the harmony of events.

Several considerations lead us to doubt whether the source of our pleasure in tragedy lies in the triumph of good over evil in the action itself. There is, to be sure, a class of tragedies in which, at the climax, the emphasis is upon a note of triumph and victory. *Faust, Romeo and Juliet,* and *The Dybbuk* are such tragedies of victory. The evil represented in the action is the separation of the lovers, and in each the climax is reached with the union of the lovers. If we were able to confine our attention to this union alone we might find in the ultimate triumph of good over evil the source of our pleasure in tragedy. But the union of the lovers is more than a mere union; it is a union in death, a union that is also a separation, a good that is also an evil. At the end of these tragedies we do not look forward to the happy future of Faust and Margaret, Romeo and Juliet, Channon and Leah, united in

6

heaven; indeed, we do not look into the future at all; we look backward over the action and feel that it brought out the good complementary to the evil represented. We accept the element of finality in the end of these characters; their destinies are completed; and we look upon the last scene as symbolic of their past rather than as prophetic of their future, finding in it the suggestion of an order that will not allow good or evil to stand alone.

There is another reason for rejecting the theory that our aesthetic pleasure arises from a happy ending, from the triumph in the action of good over evil. If this were true of the tragedies of victory, how could we account for the tragedies of defeat? Marlowe's tragedies, Shakespeare's *Macbeth,* and Ibsen's *Master Builder* proceed in a manner diametrically opposed to that of the three plays we have considered. The good for the central characters in these plays is the achievement of power, and evil for them is the loss of this power in defeat. The action of the tragedies proceeds through the development of this power to the inevitable realization of its loss; defeat furnishes the climax of each of the plays. If we follow the happy-ending theory in respect to the tragedies of victory, saying that it is the triumph of good over evil in the action which furnishes us aesthetic pleasure, we must further say that in the tragedies of defeat an exactly opposite event, the triumph of evil over good, is the source of our pleasure. Thus we should have no common theory applicable to all tragedies.

Nor can the issue be avoided by maintaining that all the spectators of the tragedies of defeat are pharisaical enough to derive their aesthetic pleasure from gloating over the downfall of a man who yielded to temptation.

7

This theory is even less flattering to the spectators of tragedy than the theory that the source of our pleasure lies in the beauty of the diction and the artistic proportions of the tragedy, a theory which implies that the spectator can bear up nobly under the sorrows of others if they are accompanied by soft music and fitting words.

If the source of our pleasure lies neither in the triumph of the artistic beauty of the tragedy over the evil in the action represented nor in the ultimate triumph of good over evil in the action itself, the justification of tragedy as a representation and as a source of aesthetic pleasure can be found only in the realization that tragedy deals with the ultimates of value, good and evil, and that approaching its task either from the side of good, as in the tragedies of defeat, or from the side of evil, as in the tragedies of victory, the action must work out and realize the complementary opposite, good or evil as the case may be, presenting it as a necessary and inevitable concomitant. Tragedy, therefore, is not a spectacle of evil; it is a spectacle of a constant and inevitable relation between good and evil, a dramatic representation of a law of values. Such is the true significance of the *metabasis,* the change of fortune. It is two-sided always, and since the climax of tragedy is always retrospective, not prophetic, our minds are fastened always on the two necessary sides of value.

The representation of this relation between good and evil is the tragic attitude toward value; and the perception of this relation, and not the good of the action itself, is the source of the spectator's pleasure; and the relation itself, which has various significances in different contexts— metaphysical, aesthetic, dramatic, and ethical—is the essential element in tragedy. It is a relation which makes itself known to feeling long before it can be expressed in a formula. The artist in tragedy does not have it in mind as a conscious goal. He experiments until he feels that he has achieved the tragic attitude; nothing else will satisfy him. Although utterly free from theory, even although guided by a false theory, he may be infallible in taste and feeling. This priority of feeling over pure knowledge holds also for the spectator and for the philosopher. The spectator must feel the effect before he can wonder at the cause, and the philosopher must recognize the tragic attitude by feeling before he can write his dissertation on the elements, intellectual content, and essence of tragedy.

It is not the function of any single tragedy to represent this relation abstractly. Tragedy is not allegorical; each tragedy deals with a specific evil and its relation to the concomitant good. It is the philosopher in thought and the spectator in feeling who transcend the particular tragedy, who generalize about the form. Feeling that this is a specific case of the universal relation between good and evil, the spectator surrenders himself to the standards and values of the tragic hero. Perhaps in his own life he could not value love as intensely as Romeo did, nor gratitude as intensely as Lear did, nor success as intensely as Macbeth did, but for the duration of the tragedies he must be a Romeo, or a Lear, or a Macbeth. Only thus can he truly witness tragedy. He must put himself into the frame of mind of the tragic hero if the tragedy is individualistic, as most of Shakespeare's are, or into the climate of opinion of an age if the tragedy represents the values of a society, as is largely true of Greek tragedy.

The most popular climate of opinion in modern tragedy is that of romantic love, in which the good of the action

9

is the union of the lovers, and the evil, consequently, their separation. Such essentially are Shakespeare's *Romeo and Juliet* and *Antony and Cleopatra,* the various versions of the Tristan and Isolde story, Ansky's *Dybbuk,* Hugo's *Hernani,* and O'Neill's *Desire Under the Elms.* Next in popularity has been the tragedy of ambition, in which good and evil are represented by power and the loss of power, as in Marlowe's tragedies, Shakespeare's *Macbeth,* and Ibsen's *Master Builder.* But the modern temper, which stresses individuality of values as opposed to the classical unity of value, gives rise to a great variety of tragic themes. Shakespeare has produced in *Hamlet,* in which the good is death and the evil is life, a tragedy which in the hands of a lesser writer would have degenerated into pessimism; in *Julius Caesar* a tragedy in which patriotism is the foreground value (of Brutus); in *Coriolanus* a tragedy of heroic pride; in *King Lear* a tragedy of gratitude and ingratitude. Virtue (in its true sense) is the foreground value in Milton's *Samson.* Goethe's *Faust* unites three climates of opinion in one tragedy; it is a tragedy of romantic love in respect to the Faust-Margaret story, a Christian tragedy in respect to the Faust-Mephistopheles story, and a third kind of tragedy, rising out of the other two, peculiarly modern in its emphasis upon the opposition between idle speculation and self-sacrificing labor.

The marked differences in themes in the history of tragedy serve, as nothing else could, to point out the element of identity in tragedy, its representation of a unique relation between good and evil. Further investigation of this relation should result in discovering the meaning of the tragic attitude toward value and the source of our pleasure in tragedy.

## II

What is the metaphysics implicit in tragedy? Viewed in this context, tragedy is significant for the relation which it suggests between good and evil abstractly considered. We may set forth several postulates clearly indicated in tragedy.

1. *Tragedy represents supplementary elements of relativity and absoluteness in values.*—Tragedy affirms a relativity of values in that it replaces the dream of a universal *summum bonum* with the recognition that goods are relative to persons and to times. The classical unity of value which held sway at the time the dream of a *summum bonum* first gained expression is a historical phenomenon which gave way to the personal values represented in Shakespeare. Yet through this very element of relativity tragedy best expresses its conception of the orderly and absolute nature of values. Every good is shown to imply its concomitant evil, and vice versa, and a constant relation is shown to exist between any and all pairs of the opposites. This absolute aspect of the problem of values is easily reached by the philosopher, who finds the tragic attitude the same in all climates of opinion. In addition, tragic artists have occasionally, by resorting to symbolism, explicitly stressed the universal applicability of their work. Ansky's *Dybbuk*, for example, which follows the tradition of the tragedy of romantic love in leaving the lovers at once united and separated at the end, is introduced and concluded by verses which apply the attitude of the tragedy to all values.

> Why, from highest height
> To deepest depth below

*11*

## Tragedy

> Has the soul fallen?
> Within itself, the Fall
> Contains the Resurrection.[1]

Tragedy is never one-sided, never falls into the error common to optimism and pessimism, never fails to see the Resurrection implied in the Fall and the Fall implied in the Resurrection. By chance or design Ansky hit upon the very symbolism used by Goethe as the final significance of *Faust*. Out of the theme of the Faust-Mephistopheles story, and out of the accompanying theme of the Faust-Margaret story, Goethe drew a meaning universally applicable to values. The two most famous quotations from the tragedy, the first from the Prologue in Heaven, the second from the last scene of Part II, make clear this application.

> While Man's desires and aspirations stir,
> He cannot choose but err.

> Whoe'er aspires unweariedly
> Is not beyond redeeming.

Often quoted, these famous statements are seldom quoted together, yet the whole attitude of the tragedy is bound up with the recognition of the relation between both. Taken alone, the first is perfectly representative of pessimism, the second, of optimism. Taken together, they represent the tragic attitude toward value. The first is not obliterated by the second; Faust may be saved, but he has erred none the less; Mephistopheles has worked good, but

---

[1] From *The Dybbuk* by S. Ansky, permission of Liveright Publishers, New York, and Henry G. Alsberg, tr. (copyright R 1953 Henry G. Alsberg and Winifred Katzin).

he has willed evil. Through symbolic stories Goethe achieved a statement of the tragic axiom.

Students of literary criticism will see in this analysis of *Faust* a solution to the controversy concerning the relation of Part I to Part II. *Faust* is a tragedy of victory with a tripartite theme. As a tragedy of victory the evils are realized first, the goods last. At the end of Part I the evils are fully realized. Through idleness and speculation Faust has erred by seeking his own selfish good; he has placed his soul within the grasp of Mephistopheles; and he has been separated from Margaret. To fulfill the need of a true tragedy the concomitant goods must be realized in Part II, and this is precisely what Goethe has brought about. Through his error Faust is brought finally to the good of self-sacrifice; this self-sacrifice makes possible his salvation from Mephistopheles; and as a final touch, he is united with Margaret in heaven. Anyone who maintains that Part I is complete as a tragedy obviously neither feels nor understands the tragic attitude.

2. *The choice of a good by the tragic hero or the dictation of a good by the classical unity of value or another climate of opinion determines the nature of the evil in the play.*—The evil will be of the same order and the exact opposite of the good. That is to say, if life is the good for the Greeks, death will be the supreme evil; if gratitude is the good for Lear, ingratitude will be the supreme evil; if power is the supreme good for Macbeth, loss of power will be the supreme evil. Simple as this may seem, it clarifies some points which have confused critics. Obviously, for example, a tragedy cannot be compounded out of the good of one climate of opinion and the evil of another. The man of successful ambition who is the victim of in-

gratitude is not a tragic figure. The romantic lover who gives up the wealth and power of the world is not a tragic figure. Nor would it be compensation to Lear to restore him to his kingdom; it is ingratitude that rankles in his soul, and only the devotion of Cordelia can set that right. That is why the many deaths in Shakespeare's tragedies are incidental to the plot, often mere parts of the mechanics of the plays. Tybalt and Paris die in the interests of the plot; the spectator is so absorbed in the efforts of the lovers to be united that he is scarcely affected. The deaths are incidental and free from the shocking and sensational character of similar incidents in older drama precisely because life is never the good in Shakespeare's great tragedies. In *Hamlet,* indeed, death itself gradually looms up as the good of the play. There are three stages in Hamlet's acceptance of death as the greatest good; the first has the force of an emotional reaction ("O, that this too, too solid flesh would melt"); the second is in the form of an intellectual query ("To be or not to be: that is the question"); and the third, summarized in his plea to Horatio not to join him in death, contains the force and audacity of absolute conviction ("If thou didst ever hold me in thy heart, Absent thee from felicity awhile"). Although an extreme case, this is probably the best study of the psychology of value yet made.

3. *According to the tragic attitude, good and evil necessarily imply one another.*—It is impossible, according to the tragic attitude, for one to find only good or only evil in life. Thus, those who see only the good or the evil of a climax of a tragedy are not truly witnessing tragedy. The culminating scenes are retrospective, not prophetic. In the tragedies of defeat these scenes are not wholly sug-

gestive of evil. Oedipus and Macbeth are fallen, but they are fallen kings. We are not allowed to forget that. Were it otherwise, we should have pathetic rather than tragic figures. In the same manner, Orestes is acquitted, but he has suffered and his sufferings are not obliterated. A most effective representation of the necessary copresence of good and evil is to be found in *The Master Builder,* where Solness, whose greatest fear is that Fortune may turn her unkindly face upon him, does not realize that by virtue of that very fear Fortune has always shown him both of her masks. And *Macbeth,* of course, is the masterly study of a fear that grows in exact proportion to the hero's triumphs.

4. *The more intensely the tragic hero appreciates the good, the more intensely will he suffer from the evil.*— This postulate meets the objection of those who feel that an Iago or an Edmund suffer no more for their villainy than do the innocent Cordelia or the honorable Othello. It is not the object of tragedy to balance the sufferings of the victims of infamy against the punishment of the infamous. The deep feelings of Othello cannot be equated with the punishment of the cold Iago, nor can the sufferings of mighty Lear be balanced by the end of the scheming and emotionally undeveloped Edmund. Only a Lear can equal a Lear; only an Othello can equal an Othello. The devotion of Cordelia rather than the deaths of Edmund and the wicked daughters compensates Lear with a feeling that is as pure and intense as was his rage at ingratitude.

The essence of tragedy, the relation it represents between good and evil, which yields these postulates when viewed metaphysically, has further significance from the point of view of aesthetics. In it we can at last be certain of the source of our pleasure in tragedy, for it removes the paradox contained in the partial analysis of tragedy as a spectacle of evil. If the essence of tragedy is that it presents evil only in order to establish an inevitable order between evil and good, then certainly this order itself, and not the evil alone, comprises the organic unity of a tragedy and the basis of aesthetic delight. But since different contexts alter the meaning of concepts, the relation between good and evil, which was simply one of necessary implication in terms of metaphysics, becomes a harmony in terms of aesthetics.

The harmony of the opposites, good and evil, which constitutes the beauty of tragedy is only one kind of that general harmony which is apparently inseparable from beauty. The harmony of music is another kind, the harmony of painting another, of poetry, another. The old definition of beauty objectively considered as unity in variety may well be condensed to its meaning of order, for harmony in its oldest philosophical sense is equivalent to fitness or order. Evils and goods, according to the tragic attitude, are not matters of chance or caprice; they are in an inevitable relation to one another; and it is this relation, this order, which delights us in tragedy, just as its equivalents delight us in the other arts. But our delight in tragedy is justifiably the most intense, for tragedies order good and evil, the values most vital to us.

## III

Since tragedy belongs primarily to the sphere of action rather than to the sphere of thought, since tragedies are to be enacted, not to be affirmed or refuted, the worth of an analysis of tragedy can only be firmly established by showing that there is an intrinsic relation between the essence of tragedy, as it is conceived in analysis, and the dramatic modes of representation common to tragedy. The question is whether the tragic artist truly represents the harmonious implication between good and evil upon the stage, and we find confirmation in (1) poetic justice, (2) tragic irony, (3) climax and denouement, and (4) plot.

1. Marlowe's *Jew of Malta*, in which the tragic hero falls into the trap he had prepared for his enemies, provides the classic example of poetic justice, a kind of symbolism which takes some mechanical device (the trap) as the mediating relation between good and evil. Barabas sees in the trap an instrument for his own greatest good; it turns out to be the instrument of his own greatest evil. Such is always the nature of poetic justice. Good and evil are linked together by some common instrument or event. The fault of the device is all too obvious. It demands a coincidence so improbable that the spectator is likely to look upon the poetic justice as a remarkable exception to the usual course of events rather than as the very law of events, a result which defeats the ends of tragedy.

2. A common dramatic device in tragedy, especially in Greek tragedy, is that of tragic irony. Oedipus, at the height of his power, denounces in terrible terms the unknown murderer, who the audience knows is Oedipus himself. Again, the customarily morbid and cheerless Romeo, banished to Mantua, has a vision of future success at a time when the audience knows that a messenger is already on the way to tell him of Juliet's death. The success of tragic irony is apparent, for it places the good and the evil in the life of the tragic hero in the mind of

the spectator at one time, emphasizing their relation to one another. But, on account of its momentary nature, it is a limited form of representation, a fleeting revelation of the truth.

3. At the denouement of Hugo's *Hernani* the two lovers are at last alone together. Their supreme good is in the foreground, and there apparently is no background (*"Pas un nuage au ciel"*). At this very moment they hear the horn which is the signal that Hernani must die; the background of evil supplements the foreground of good, and the tragic effect is realized. The climactic scenes of tragedy, as we have noted, commonly affirm this tragic effect. The impression of the fallen is that they are fallen kings, of the dead and separated lovers that they are in some sense united. The ironic climax is a common device. At the climax of the *Electra* of Sophocles, Aegisthus joyfully uncovers what he believes to be the body of his enemy, Orestes, but finds instead the body of Clytemnestra. Again, the Emperor Jones, who regards his silver bullet as a charm, is finally killed by the revolting natives, who use silver bullets.

4. Effective as these devices are in representing the necessary copresence of good and evil, they suffer from their momentary character; and for this reason the dianoetic element in tragedy, its essence, is best represented in the plot. Since the play must represent an inevitable order of values if it is to reach the tragic effect, the plot alone, or the totality of the action represented, can support the representation of eternal law. Minor dramatic devices may seem upon second thought to be exceptions to the law of values, but that which is firmly rooted in the plot seems to flow from the metaphysical essence of the

world itself. And it is, of course, a commonplace since Aristotle that tragic plots contain the *metabasis*, the change of fortune, which represents the relation between good and evil. Perhaps the best comparative test of the worth of a tragedy is the degree of skill with which this inevitable relation between good and evil in the life of the tragic hero is set forth in the unfolding of the plot. The plot of *Hedda Gabler*, for instance, is divided into two stages, each representing the relation between good and evil. In the first stage the tragic heroine, striving desperately to bring about her supreme good, brings about her greatest evil; in the second stage this evil in turn brings about her supreme good. Hedda Gabler, decadent aristocrat, is reduced by marriage to a middle-class life; the circumstances are such that she can escape, without compromising her peculiar standards, only by death. Lacking courage for this action, her mind becomes fixed upon the hope of vicarious satisfaction; Lövberg's death by his own hand will bring one moment of aristocratic beauty into her life. But his death, in which she co-operates, has the opposite effect in realizing extreme ugliness. Her reaction to this ugliness is so violent that she is at last able to end her own life, an act of which she was incapable at the beginning of the action.

This quality in the successful tragic plot, its dramatization of the dianoetic element of tragedy, is common to the play that observes the dramatic unities and to the play fashioned with an almost formless technique. Milton's *Samson Agonistes* observes the dramatic unities, but it owes its true unity as a tragedy to the unity of the action in which Samson, in the supreme triumph of his virtue or strength, brings about its end in death. The apparent formlessness of *King Lear,* on the other hand, can be shown to be an essential element in the perfect plot of the greatest of all tragedies. The creator of *King Lear,* in order to represent the inevitable relation between good and evil, must show that Lear, a man of tremendous intensity of feeling, who has chosen his relation with his children as his chief value, will inevitably experience the extremes of value. How is this accomplished dramatically? As a visible sign of his choice of values, Lear plans to divide his kingdom among his children, asking in return only a manifestation of their affection. As it happens, Cordelia, from whom he expects most, is able, as a woman of action rather than of words, to show least. After Cordelia is disinherited and banished, Lear's extreme evil is soon realized by the ingratitude and cruelty of Goneril and Regan, which drive Lear to his first great intensity of feeling. But this evil (and here lies the genius of the plot) immediately implies its opposite, for it opens the only road which could make it possible for Cordelia to show her true feeling. Returning from France, she sacrifices first her freedom, ultimately her life, for her father. And it is the intensity of feeling aroused by her love which accompanies Lear to his death.

In this manner we find the tragic essence reflected in poetic justice, tragic irony, climax and denouement, plot, and all the dramatic devices, major or minor, appropriate to tragedy.

Tragedy, through the necessities of dramatic representation, differs from life in many ways. Tragedy is selective; it chooses out of the usual neutral gray of everyday life some colorful opposition between good and evil and makes the achievement of the harmony of these opposites its aesthetic goal. It provides a dramatic heightening, a concentration, and a finality not often found in everyday experience. Tragedies always rise to the heroic level; life seldom does. Yet the axioms that we read through its dramatic modes of representation are plainly based on an inevitable order of values, an order which obtains on every level of living, heroic or otherwise.

Indeed, looking through the outward form of tragedy to its inner axioms, we come to look upon the heroic element as an adjunct to dramatic representation. The law of values represented in tragedy is for plain people as well as for heroes, and tragedy, a representation of life, reflects upon the process of living itself. The tragic essence, which yields the metaphysical axioms of value, the secret of our aesthetic pleasure, and the meaning of the dramatic modes, has a further significance in terms of the conduct of life. The metaphysical implication between good and evil, which in aesthetic terms is a harmony constituting the beauty of tragedy, becomes in ethical terms a justice constituting the truth of everyday experience and the meaning of life in terms of good and evil.

If this be so, how does tragedy function as material for a philosophy of values? First, it is evident that the essence of tragedy, representing as it does an inevitable relation between good and evil, satisfies the principle of such a philosophy that values must be subject to law, and not to chance, caprice, or fortune. Second, tragedy meets the further principle of a philosophy of values in that the order which it represents is something more than the blank necessity which characterizes impersonal disciplines. The general order of the world, tragedy indicates, has a specific and personal meaning in terms of good and evil. It is not enough to say, confining ourselves to metaphysical terms, that a necessary implication exists between good and evil. In the light of aesthetic problems that necessary implication is a harmony which is the source of our pleasure; and in the light of problems of conduct that necessary implication is a justice which gives warmth and value to eternal law itself.

Some indication of the manner in which true tragedy affirms the two necessary principles of a philosophy of values may be found in a comparison of the *Oresteia* of Aeschylus with the modern imitation by O'Neill, *Mourning Becomes Electra*. In the Aeschylean trilogy an inevitable order of values is indicated by the sequence of tragic events, a sequence rooted in the very beginnings of the foredoomed halls of the house of Atreus. Aegisthus avenges his father, and Clytemnestra, her daughter, Iphigenia, in the death of Agamemnon. Orestes, in turn, avenges the death of Agamemnon in the deaths of Clytemnestra and Aegisthus, and in turn the Furies of Clytemnestra pursue Orestes. O'Neill has displayed an almost point-by-point fidelity to the original in building a modern parallel. With necessary differences in motivation, Orin and Lavinia replace Orestes and Electra, Christine and Brant replace Clytemnestra and Aegisthus, and Mannon replaces Agamemnon. The same inevitability is suggested in an analogous sequence of events. Up to this point *Mourning Becomes Electra* is a successful imitation, but O'Neill is unable to follow Aeschylus in establishing the second principle of a philosophy of values. Aeschylus is not content with the mere orderly sequence of values; his culminating task is to represent the nature of the order of values. This he accomplishes through what is for us symbolism. The sequence of events is broken by the trial of

Orestes, at which justice obtains in the acquittal of Orestes and the appeasement of the Furies. The inevitable order of human values makes manifest a justice ordained by the gods. Into this symbolic realm O'Neill cannot safely follow, and as his tragedy ends, we know nothing more than that the orderly sequence will be carried out to the bitter end, that, as Lavinia turns back into the house, we have come to the last link in the chain of necessary events. The chain remains a chain, and O'Neill's tragedy, because it can furnish nothing to replace the symbolism of the older trilogy, remains in a pre-Aeschylean attitude toward values; values are ruled by stern necessity, but that necessity is not seen in its true light as justice.

By its interpretation of the eternal law of values as justice tragedy places itself under the unity of Western culture. Whether it be as a representation of life or as artistic addition, only in the category of justice have the poet, the philosopher, and the religious teacher rested content with the meaning of life. Thus it had been with Homer, Heraclitus, and Aeschylus; and after Plato turned from the life of the individual to the activities of the state in search of justice, Christianity swept over him and over Greek philosophy, subordinating them to its vision. For beneath the softer surface of Christianity, Augustine and Thomas found that durable skeleton of eternal justice which has been represented in art by Dante and Milton; and this central thread of Greek and medieval culture still runs through the modern *Weltanschauung,* as we discover in Leibniz's theodicy, Hegel's philosophy of history, Emerson's theory of compensation, and Whitman's *Leaves of Grass.*     ·

But the very concept of justice is in its development the

product of creative imagination, and poets and tragic artists have been the largest contributors to its elaboration and perfection. The common conception of justice as a balance or equilibrium derives from the conception behind the picture of the golden scales of Zeus in the *Iliad*. From this conception all theories of justice start and diverge according to the notions of how the equilibrium is achieved. Tragedy is rich in such diverging conceptions, ranging from the poetic justice which we have found to be a minor dramatic device through the symbolism of Greek tragedy to its most important contribution to a philosophy of value, the unique conception of justice latent in the dianoetic background of tragic art.

In its search for the meaning of justice tragedy concerns itself with the individual rather than with the political animal of Aristotle, a point which clearly differentiates tragedy from the social-problem play. No matter how much the action of the plot may be related to social conditions or political or economic events, the attitude of tragedy clearly is that the citizen is merely a limited aspect of the man. The tragic hero may or may not follow the bent of his society; some yield to Caesar, and others, like Antigone, are guided by another law.

The tragic attitude toward material things is identical with its attitude toward the state. The individual works out his destiny through social institutions and through material things, but it is he, and not these things, who is the center of gravity in the problem of values. Societies and things have value only insofar as they are valued, only insofar as they enter into the lives of individuals. This is indicated by the climates of opinion in tragedy and established by the axioms of relativity (Axioms 1, 2).

The inevitable order in things valued exists only by virtue of the inevitable order in the individual's capacity to value (Axioms 3, 4).

It is this preoccupation with the values of the individual that makes tragedy necessary material for a philosophy of value. The methodology of philosophy is invaluable in solving certain problems in the realm of values, but methodology, on account of its impersonal nature, must be applied to the arts of personal feeling before the true nature of values can be fully grasped. There is contained in the dramatic modes of representation in tragedy something indigenous to the form—a unique conception of eternal justice in terms of individuals—which cannot be discovered elsewhere.

This conception of justice is not consonant with the notion of justice at the level of the *lex talionis,* the law of the claw, for, as we have seen, tragedy recognizes the impossibility of exacting an eye for an eye, of bringing upon the emotionally undeveloped Edmund and Iago sorrows as great as those of Othello and Lear. Indeed, its conception is not in agreement with any of the traditional notions of either distributive or retributive justice. Because it is artistically self-sufficient, never carrying the spectator beyond the action, and because its climax is always retrospective, it cannot admit the eternal justice of rewards and punishments represented in Dante. There is in it no question of the distribution of material goods for the achievement of justice, for such goods are meaningless to an Oedipus, a Lear, an Antigone.

Tragedy has been led by the inequality of men to reject the concepts of justice at these levels. The feelings of one individual can seldom, perhaps never, be duplicated;

hence the exaction of an eye for an eye is impossible; hence the equal distribution of goods is not a just government of values. A just government of values could only obtain by so regulating the individual's capacity for feeling that it would carry with it his fate and the justice of his life. Tragedy proclaims a law effecting this just government of values. Although, in the realm of values, no two men are equal in respect either to capacity for feeling or to choice of values, each individual is exactly equal to himself, and the eternal justice which cannot be found in attempting to equate Othello with Iago or Lear with Goneril and Regan can be found in the observation that an Othello is exactly equal to himself and a Lear exactly equal to himself. Operating through the two-sided nature of value (Axiom 3), eternal justice is manifest in the perfect measure governing the life of the individual (Axiom 4). Romeo, Solness, Orestes, Hedda, Iago, Faust, and Channon are all unequal in capacity for feeling and choice of values, but one and the same law of values orders inevitably the good and the evil in the life of each.

This conception of justice, which is the essential contribution of tragedy to the philosophy of values, rejects the moral law at the levels of the *lex talionis* and the theories of distribution and retribution, but it affirms the moral law on the plane where virtue is taken to be its own reward. The nicety of the tragic law is such that the piety and love of virtue of Antigone are sufficient psychologically to motivate her tragic action, just as Samson's need to exercise his virtue overcomes the psychological obstacle contained in the tragic fact that in exercising it he will bring it to an end in death.

Following the tradition which conceives of the notions

of equilibrium, balance, and equality as lying at the center of the idea of justice, tragedy denies that this equality can be found in the relation of the citizen to the state (as in Plato's *Republic*), or in the relation between individual and individual (as in the *lex talionis*), but affirms that it can be found in the relation of the individual to himself, in his perfect self-equality. The equality of good and evil which constitutes justice can be found only in the individual, whose capacity for experiencing good is exactly equal to his capacity for experiencing evil.

It is perhaps well to note that an intellectual grasp of this tragic attitude is an invaluable supplement to tragedy rather than a substitute for it, for tragedy, as an experience, constantly reminds us that the law of values, abstracted and formulated by philosophy, is only an intellectual reflection of the lives and actions of individuals.

# II ☆

# Aristotle's Study

# of Tragedy

THE *Poetics* of Aristotle, which contains the best-known definition of tragedy, has been more lavishly praised and more bitterly condemned than any other work of literary criticism. These extremes of judgment seem to be founded on a common misunderstanding: friend and foe alike have erred in treating Aristotle as a prophet and lawgiver rather than as a scientist and philosopher. Those who have praised the *Poetics* most highly have often revealed their ignorance of the scientific method upon which it is based by accepting Aristotle's findings as though they were oracles from on high, and those who have most bitterly condemned the *Poetics* have done so because they have mistakenly ascribed to Aristotle the dogmatism which is all too evident in the writings of some of his disciples.

I

The outstanding merit of the *Poetics,* the quality which makes it the necessary starting point of any inquiry into the nature of tragedy, is its application of a scientific method to the study of poetry. This method is more important than the particular conclusions which have inspired so much fruitless controversy. Among its procedures are the use of inductive reasoning, the analysis of specimens into their constituent elements or parts, and the synthesizing of conclusions in a definition by genus and differentiae. Of these, the most important is induction, the mode of reasoning which derives general propositions from a careful study of particular instances. If any of Aristotle's generalizations concerning tragedy are valid, they owe their validity to the fact that before formulating them he examined the tragedies available in his time as carefully as a botanist examines a collection of rare plants.

A generalization which is supported by all the known facts or instances is incontestable and may properly be regarded as scientific description. If all the tragedies with which we are familiar had been available to Aristotle, we may be sure that he would have taken them into account and that as a result the *Poetics,* greatly modified, would be for us a much more satisfactory and accurate description of the general nature of tragedy. But he had only the Greek tragedies, including the many now lost and the few that have survived, to study; and he himself implies that his conclusions may be tentative by raising the question "whether tragedy has as yet perfected its proper types."

It had not yet perfected all its possible types, as we

know; and for this reason the *Poetics* is for us a compilation of conclusions which are based on incomplete evidence. We may determine whether these conclusions need to be modified by carefully examining the new types and examples of tragedy, or we may accept them as they stand because they are the dicta of an eminent philosopher. If we accept only those generalizations which are supported by the facts, we follow Aristotle in the use of inductive reasoning, his chief contribution to the study of literature; if we accept his findings as dicta, we turn from scientific description to literary prescription, to a kind of a priori critical authoritarianism which is the exact opposite of the Aristotelian method.

The excellence of Aristotle's method cannot make up for the outstanding weakness of his study, namely, his indifference to the meaning of tragedy and his consequent failure to trace the general outlines of the tragic view of life. This failure of a great philosopher to judge, or even to notice, an important view of life can only be explained as an aftereffect of that "ancient quarrel between philosophy and poetry" which Socrates describes to Glaucon in Plato's *Republic*. The cause of the quarrel was the desire of the philosophers to replace the poets as the sole interpreters of life and as the recognized teachers in questions of conduct. Since the Greeks were unique among early peoples in their freedom from a priestly caste, their poets enjoyed for many centuries, and particularly from the time of Homer to the time of Euripides, a secure prestige as recorders and interpreters of experience and tradition. When the early Greek philosophers turned from the study of nature to the study of man, however, they encroached upon the preserves of the poets, and the resulting rivalry reached a peak of intensity at the end of the fifth century B.C. Aristophanes presents a bitterly satirical picture of Socrates in *The Clouds;* and Plato, using Socrates as spokesman, strikes back hard at the poets in the *Republic.* Poetry, he maintains, is thrice removed from the truth since the poet copies a particular object which in turn is a copy of a universal idea. Many of the best-known poems contain immoral fictions which represent gods and heroes as even worse in behavior than ordinary men. The pleasures afforded by poetry are at best of an inferior order; at worst they may lead men into weak sentimentalism or buffoonery. Poetry feeds the passions, which should be starved. For these and other reasons Plato would expel the poets from his ideal republic.

Aristotle's attitude toward the poets is so much less uncompromising than Plato's that he seems at first glance to do justice to the significance of poetry. Writing at a time when the philosophers had gained in prestige at the expense of their rivals, he is generous in victory and seeks to end the ancient quarrel by assigning to the poets a respected sphere of activity and to poetry an important function. The true end of poetry, he maintains, is to give pleasure, and the pleasure derived from poetry is a good which contributes to the well-being of the virtuous man. The effect of great poetry upon the emotions is beneficial, not injurious. As for the fictions of the poets, they are dangerous only to children, who cannot distinguish between fiction and fact; for mature men the poet is an artist and not a teacher, and the appeal of poetry is to the feelings and not to the intellect.

While conceding to the poet an important role as a contributor to the emotional well-being of man, Aristotle reserves to the philosopher the more important function of interpreting life. This division of functions between the rivals has merit. By stressing the fact that the reading of poetry has a value apart from any moral guidance which may be found in the experience, it helps the critic to distinguish a poem from a didactic jingle. But it implies a sharp division between the intellect and the emotions which does not in fact exist. Our reason and our feelings are not shut up in separate compartments; on the contrary, our feelings are stirred solely by our ideas, and our ideas are all too often inspired solely by feeling. The feelings which inspire a system of philosophy and the intellectual pattern of a poem may be implicit rather than explicit; but they are present, and not to be ignored. If a tragic drama has the power to restore us to tranquillity after stirring our deepest feelings, the reason is that the poet has shaped his tragic incidents into a pattern, implicitly intellectual, which we are usually unable to discover when similar incidents occur as parts of the chaos of everyday experience. The question whether that pattern is the true pattern of human life is the most important question concerning tragedy, but it is a question that we are not likely to raise if we assign the realm of feeling to the poet and the realm of ideas to the philosopher.

Aristotle seems to have been at least partly aware that the power of poetry to excite and soothe our feelings implies that poetry has intellectual aspects of a high order. Poetry, he tells us, is higher and more philosophical than history, for poetry stresses the universal while history stresses the particular. This recognition of the universality of poetry might well have raised the essential question concerning tragedy in Aristotle's mind, for if poetry tends to express the universal, the tragic hero may truly represent mankind, and his fate may be the fate of all men. If not, why not? But Aristotle is too deeply committed to his solution of the ancient quarrel to probe deeply into the intellectual patterns implicit in poetry. An examination of the high points of the *Poetics*—the analysis of tragedy into its elements, the description of the ideal tragic hero, and the famous definition of tragedy—reveals that, in spite of his excellent method of investigation, he never credits the tragic poet with an important view of life and is content to explain, as best he can, how tragedy affords intense pleasure by exciting and purging the emotions of pity and fear.

## II

The constituent elements of tragedy, according to Aristotle, are, in their order of importance, plot, character, thought, diction, melody, and spectacle. By plot he means the structure of the story which is unfolded in dramatic action, the organization of the incidents which provides the pattern and unity of the tragedy. By character (*ethos*) he does not mean an individual agent in a tragedy, as Agamemnon or Romeo; he means the moral bent which disposes an Agamemnon or a Romeo to choose or avoid a certain course of action. His illustrations of thought (*dianoia*) refer to passages in which speakers use rhetoric to excite feeling, offer arguments in proof or disproof of a point, or use general maxims in commenting upon events; thought, therefore, means either the intellectual ability of a speaker, his skill in saying the right thing at the right time, or examples of this ability. By diction Aristotle means the poet's choice and arrangement of words; by melody he means the choral songs of Greek tragedy; and by spectacle he means the costuming and scenery required in the theatrical production of a tragedy.

Aristotle's treatment of thought, which is consistent with his solution to the rivalry between the poets and the philosophers, is the principal defect in his analysis of tragedy into its constituent elements. Since he is convinced in advance that the proper appeal of poetry is to the emotions, he ignores the tragic view of life implied in the possibility that the hero's fate may truly represent the destiny of man. His thought—the intellectual ability of the hero or of other agents as evidenced by their skill in persuasion, in argumentation, and in the use of apposite maxims—is too narrow a conception to throw much light upon the over-all meaning of tragedy.

Since the intellectual ability of an agent may play as important a part as his moral bent in disposing him to choose or avoid a certain course of action, we might well treat intellectual ability and moral bent as two aspects of character, thereby eliminating Aristotle's thought and making room for the element of tragedy which he ignores, namely, meaning. For plot, character, and meaning are in fact the principal elements of tragedy, and their interdependence and equal importance may best be indicated by a simple formula: plot plus character equals meaning.

For Aristotle, however, plot is the first element of tragedy, and his discussion of its importance is a masterly combination of analysis and induction. A well-constructed plot, he tells us, has a beginning, a middle, and an end; and the series of incidents which it comprises follow one another in a probable or inevitable sequence, forming an organic whole. It is neither too short to be impressive nor too long for its parts to be easily held in memory; within these limits its precise length is best determined by the number of incidents necessary to represent a change from bad fortune to good, or from good fortune to bad.

The relative effectiveness of plots, according to the *Poetics,* may be explained by an analysis of their construction. The worst plots are the episodic, in which the episodes or events follow one another without probable or necessary sequence. An effective plot, on the other hand, always represents a single action, a change of fortune in which no incident may be displaced or removed without disturbing the organic unity of the whole. The best plots combine change of fortune (*metabasis*) with reversal (*peripeteia*) and discovery (*anagnorisis*). Change of fortune is a series of events in probable or necessary sequence carrying the hero from prosperity to adversity, or from adversity to prosperity—as the downfall of Oedipus in *Oedipus the King,* or his restoration to the favor of the gods in *Oedipus at Colonus.* Reversal is a change by which a course of action results in the opposite of the effect intended by the agent—as in *Oedipus the King* the Messenger intends to cheer Oedipus and free him from his fears by revealing his identity but instead hastens his fall into misery. Discovery is a change from ignorance to knowledge, and the most effective discovery, Aristotle concludes, is a recognition of identity accompanied by a reversal and a change of fortune, as in *Oedipus the King.*

Nothing in the later history of drama discredits Aristotle's main observations on the parts of plot. Forms of drama to which his generalizations are inapplicable have appeared and enjoyed popularity, but only the hazier critics have mistaken these new forms for tragedy. The slice-of-life play, of which Gorki's *Lower Depths* is the archetype, always represents many actions instead of one action and often derives its unity mainly from its setting. The expressionistic play, stemming from Strindberg's *Dream Play* and *Spook Sonata,* is composed of episodes which usually follow one another in a kaleidoscopic or dreamlike fashion quite unlike the probable or necessary sequence which events follow in the plots of effective tragedies. But Gorki, Strindberg, and their followers have artistic aims different from the aims of such artists in tragedy as Aeschylus, Shakespeare, Goethe, Ibsen, and O'Neill; and their slice-of-life and expressionistic plays, when subjected to the Aristotelian method of study, reveal new principles of construction peculiarly suited to the achievement of the new aims. The emotional and intellectual effects of tragedy, however, still depend upon the sense of inevitability which the tragic dramatist conveys to the reader or spectator by unfolding the events of his plot in a probable or necessary sequence.

The later history of drama fully supports Aristotle's observation that change of fortune is the indispensable element of a tragic plot, and that the best plots combine a change of fortune with a reversal and a discovery. The best discoveries in later tragedies, it is true, do not always depend upon recognition of personal identity, as Aristotle thinks they should; but although the discoveries of the Elizabethan or modern hero may be intangible truths or values, they are nevertheless correctly described by his general definition of discovery as a change from ignorance to knowledge. Similarly, although Sophocles prefers to use only a half-turn of the great wheel of fortune in each tragedy, representing the fall of Oedipus in one play and his subsequent rise in another, Shakespeare prefers a full turn of the wheel, representing in single plays the fall and rise of Lear and the rise and fall of Macbeth. These minor changes do not affect the validity of Aristotle's analysis of plot; and anyone who examines the plots of *King Lear,* of *Faust,* of *Hedda Gabler,* and of *Desire Under the Elms* will find that, like the plot of *Oedipus the King,* their effectiveness mainly depends upon an artful combination of a change of fortune with a reversal and a discovery.

The more we are impressed by the brilliance of Aristotle's analysis of plot, however, the more we must be disappointed by his failure to expand his findings into a description of the tragic view of life. Since he asserts without reservation that plot is the soul of tragedy, its animating principle, and since he considers the manner in which the incidents of the best plots mirror the events of life, we might expect that if ever he is to pose the question of the over-all meaning of tragedy, he will do so at this point in his discussion. Significantly, at this point we do find his famous assertion that poetry is more philosophical than history in that it stresses the universal rather than the particular.

Aristotle persists, however, in treating even the plot of his favorite tragedy as though its values were chiefly or altogether emotional. That *Oedipus the King* was his favorite we may infer from his comments on its qualities: he mentions Oedipus first in a list of personages suitable for treatment in perfect tragedies, and from the plot of the play he derives his first example of reversal and his first example of the best kind of discovery. Yet he analyzes the perfections of its plot only because they heighten the feelings excited by the downfall of Oedipus; the plot is so

admirably constructed, he tells us, that a reader, or one
who hears the play read, will experience the same in-
tensities of pity and fear which affect one who sees the
play enacted, with costuming and scenery, in the theatre.

How stultifying a preoccupation with the emotional
effects of tragedy can be is evident from the fact that Aristotle fails to mention the reversal and the discovery which
most clearly indicate the profound meaning of *Oedipus
the King*. As his example of reversal, he instances the recoil whereby the Messenger's attempt to cheer Oedipus
produces the opposite effect, a recoil which is accompanied by his example of the best kind of discovery, the
recognition by Oedipus of his true identity as the son of
Laius and Jocasta. This combination is indeed emotionally
exciting, but in the most wonderfully intricate of all plots
it is merely a move toward the revelation of the best of all
combinations. The supreme reversal in the tragedy is the
recoil of events whereby Oedipus, who fled from Corinth
to evade the oracle that he will kill his father and marry
his mother, brings on his doom by his efforts to escape.
The discovery which accompanies this supreme reversal
is that he who seeks to evade the inevitable merely hastens
its fulfillment, a proposition as profoundly significant as
any in science or philosophy and more convincingly
demonstrated than most. To Oedipus, who at the end
accepts the oracle as the will of the gods, this discovery is
proof of his own responsibility for his fate; to the spectator
who no longer believes in oracles it is nevertheless a light
thrown upon the nature of whatever he accepts as the inevitable; but to Aristotle it is apparently a discovery in a
realm in which the poet lacks authority.

When we seriously consider the tendency of poetry to

express the universal, we find in tragedy, and particularly in the parts of plot, an intellectually significant pattern which Aristotle overlooked. If poetry stresses the universal, then surely change of fortune, the indispensable part of the first element of tragedy, represents the fundamental condition of life, the essence of human destiny: good and evil are the necessary poles of experience, and no man may hope to enjoy life without paying the price in suffering. The main reversal in a great tragedy demonstrates that this fundamental condition of life is unalterable: when the hero attempts to evade it, an inevitable recoil of events hastens his fall into misery. Finally, the important discovery in every great tragedy is the revelation to the hero of some meaning in his fate and to the spectator of some of the fixed and universal conditions of human destiny.

### III

Aristotle considers five basic situations, involving various kinds of persons in changes of fortune, as possible material for tragic plots, rejecting the first three, praising the fourth as suitable for a perfect tragedy, and describing the fifth as a concession to the inferior taste of theatregoers. (1) On two grounds he rejects the fall of a virtuous man from prosperity to adversity: first, it excites neither pity nor fear, and secondly, it is revolting to our moral sense. (2) Similarly, he rejects the rise of a bad man from adversity to prosperity because it neither satisfies the moral sense nor excites pity and fear. (3) On a single ground, however, he rejects the downfall of an utterly wicked man: although it satisfies the moral sense, it is neither pitiable nor terrible. (4) After these rejections there remains, he tells us, as intermediate between these extremes, the man, neither vicious and depraved nor eminently virtuous and just, whose misfortune is brought on by some failure (*hamartia*) to find the path of wise and virtuous conduct. This situation is ideal, he maintains, for the downfall of such a man excites the pity which we feel for one whose great misfortune is unmerited and the terror which we feel in witnessing the misfortune of a man like ourselves. And presumably—although Aristotle does not say so—his change of fortune also satisfies our moral sense. (5) As a concession to the weakness of the audience, however, the dramatist often chooses a story with a double thread of plot, in which the good personages rise and the bad fall. This is an inferior kind of drama, and more like comedy than tragedy.

Aristotle's description of the ideal tragic hero as an intermediate between the extremes of the eminently virtuous man and the utterly depraved man is confirmed by the distinction which we now make between melodrama and tragedy. In the black-and-white world of melodrama men are divided into two sharply opposed classes, represented by the unblemished hero and the unspeakable villain. In tragedy, however, the hero whose deeds match his intentions in goodness and the villain whose deeds reflect his evil intentions disappear and are replaced by a single representative of mankind, a man whose intentions are always good, but whose judgment of what is the good for himself and for others is clouded by the urgencies of his appetites and passions. The first premise of melodrama is that there are two distinct kinds of men: the first premise of tragedy is that all men are essentially the same. That the *Poetics* foreshadows this distinction is evident from the fact that Aristotle rejects as unsuitable for tragedy all changes of fortune (1, 2, 3, 5) involving melodramatic heroes and villains.

The changes of fortune which Aristotle rejects are not, however, all suitable for melodrama. Although they all involve either eminently virtuous or utterly vicious men, only two of them (3, 5) provide a conclusion agreeable to our ingrained sense of justice. The first premise of melodrama may misrepresent the facts of life, but once it is accepted, it renders all conclusions save one unacceptable to our moral sense; consequently, every effective melodrama ends in the poetic justice which rewards the innocent and punishes the guilty. Since they indicate that injustice prevails, the downfall of a good man (1) and the rise of a bad man (2) are effective in drama only as the bases for the problem and propaganda plays which incite the spectator to take action against the *status quo* in society. The overthrow of a villain (3) satisfies the demands of poetic justice, but since a villain's defeat is usually a hero's victory, the story with a double thread of plot, with appropriate rewards and punishments for the innocent and the guilty (5), is always the most effective material for popular melodrama.

How does tragedy itself satisfy our ingrained love of justice? Aristotle does not answer this question. Moreover, since his ethical views are set forth in detail in the *Nichomachean Ethics,* he does not trouble in the *Poetics* to analyze or define the failure (*hamartia*) which he describes as the immediate cause of the hero's misfortune. Some interpreters of the *Poetics* have reduced tragedy to the level of melodrama by insisting that the hero's *hamartia* is a sin, and that our pleasure in tragedy is partly derived from our discovery of a condign punishment in the hero's downfall. The available evidence clearly indicates, however, that Aristotle found in tragedy a pleasure different from the pleasure afforded to moralizers by an instance of poetic justice. First, he attributes the pity properly excited by the best tragedies to the spectacle of a misfortune greater than the fault which is its cause. Secondly, he describes the best possible illustration of poetic justice (5) as a concession to the weakness of spectators. Finally, it is most unlikely that he, the author of the *Nichomachean Ethics,* could have failed to understand the true nature of the tragic hero's *hamartia.*

The final test of the good life, of happiness as it is described in the *Nichomachean Ethics,* is completeness. Happiness or well-being (*eudaimonia*), the true aim of life, is to be found only in complete self-realization, in full participation in the activities proper to a human being. As eye, hand, foot, and all parts of the body have specific functions, and as the musician, the sculptor, and the artist have each a distinct function, so man must have a function which distinguishes him from other beings. This function cannot be merely living, for the life of nutrition and growth is shared even by plants; it cannot be life at the level of perception, for perception is a function of all animals. Consequently, the true function of man must be activity which follows or implies a rational principle, for man is the only rational animal. The function of the good man is to perform in a great and noble manner activities involving reason: happiness may be found only in activity of soul in accordance with virtue. But, Aristotle tells us, the happy life is a complete life. One swallow does not make a summer, nor does one day; and one day, or a short time, does not make a man happy.

The good life requires moderation in those spheres of activity in which reason must co-operate with the appetites and passions. Here we must always aim at the golden mean which lies between the extremes of too little and too much, at the courage which is the mean between the extremes of cowardice and rashness, at the proper pride which lies between abject humility and vanity, at the temperance which lies between abstinence and indulgence, at the liberality which lies between miserliness and extravagance, at the friendliness which lies between surliness and obsequiousness. But since acts involving moral choice are always particular events, the mean between too little and too much is always relative to the facts of a particular situation; consequently, its determination is no easy task.

Aristotle discusses important exceptions to his doctrines of the golden mean and the complete life. An exception to the doctrine of the golden mean is that no mean between too little and too much can be found in respect to certain passions and acts; as their names indicate, such passions as spite, shamelessness, and envy and such actions as adultery, theft, and murder are always bad. One cannot, for example, make adultery right by moderation, by committing it only with the right woman, at the right time, and in the right way: it is always wrong. An exception to the doctrine of the complete life is that the doing of an unquestionably noble deed may be compensation for the loss of a complete life. If necessary, the good man will cheerfully sacrifice his life for his friend or for his country, for he will prefer one great and noble deed to many petty activities, and one year lived nobly to many years spent in routine affairs.

In respect to the moral virtues the *Nichomachean Ethics* is a philosophical refinement of the common sense which is based upon experience, particularly of that kind of common sense which evaluates the passing moment by the long view rather than the short view. Long before Aristotle, some sensible man coined the adage that one swallow does not make a summer, and generations of sensible men have since repeated it to make the point that a momentary pleasure may not lead to lifelong happiness. Like Aristotle, the sensible man condemns those acts which everywhere have a bad name and praises those acts which are everywhere regarded as noble. The moral problems of the sensible man are not raised by clear cases of vice and virtue; they arise when he is confronted by the particular situations which require him to choose the mean between too little and too much, to discover the moderate course most likely to lead to the long and complete life which he prizes above all else. In short, Aristotle, the philosopher of common sense, is altogether worldly in the best sense of the word: his object is to attain the good here and now, not in the hereafter; his conception of the good includes the life of the appetites and passions as well as the life of reason; and his means of attaining the good, insofar as problems of moral virtue are involved, is chiefly the moderation which experience has proved the best course for one who aims at a long and complete life.

How, then, would the author of the *Nichomachean Ethics* regard the tragic hero and his *hamartia*? First, we must remember that for Aristotle the ideal tragic hero is not one whose misfortune is brought on by a vice which is everywhere regarded as a vice, nor is he one whose change of fortune consists in his laying down his life for his friend or for his country, or in any similar act of unquestionable nobility. But if he is neither utterly depraved nor eminently virtuous, what is his outstanding trait? As we meet him in the world's great tragedies, he is, first and foremost, an extremist. To reach his goal, whatever it may be, he is always willing to sacrifice everything else, including his life. Oedipus will press the search for the unknown murderer, although he is warned of the consequences; Hamlet will prove the King's guilt and attempt to execute perfect justice, whatever the cost may be to his mother, to Laertes, to Ophelia, and to himself; Solness will climb the tower he has built, at the risk of falling into the quarry; Ahab will kill Moby Dick or die in the attempt. The usual consequence of this heroic extremism is exactly what experience has taught the sensible man to expect: the tragic hero lives intensely but not long—his summer often ends with the first swallow. If we judge him by the standards of the ordinary sensible man, he fails, through a lack of moderation, to realize the supreme good of a long and complete life. And it is doubtless this failure which Aristotle has in mind when he ascribes the tragic hero's misfortune to his *hamartia*.

But although Aristotle correctly describes the ideal tragic hero, he fails to explain what John Dewey has called "the peculiar power of tragedy to leave us at the end with a sense of reconciliation rather than with one of horror." That tragedy has this power to make us feel that the conditions of life are as just as they are ineluctable countless other witnesses have testified. At points in the unfolding of a great tragedy we experience the pity and terror which, as Aristotle maintains, the misfortunes of men like ourselves normally excite, but these and other deep feelings which we experience as we follow the hero in his moments of glory and despair are at the end merged with our recognition of a pattern in the hero's fate into a total impression as significant as it is moving. And since meaning is as important a part of this total impression as feeling, a philosopher who limits his study of poetry to its emotional effects can never adequately explain the wonderful power of tragedy.

If we analyze those intellectual aspects of the total impression of tragedy which Aristotle neglects, we find that the ideal tragic hero's change of fortune may satisfy our sense of justice in at least three important ways. First of all, we discover in the intensity of the hero's experience a compensation for its lack of breadth and duration. As Aristotle points out in the *Nichomachean Ethics*, the good man who lays down his life for his friend prefers the intense satisfaction of a single noble deed to years of dull existence. The ideal tragic hero is not an eminently virtuous man, but he too prefers drinking the cup of life at a single draught to taking it in the manner of a valetudinarian sipping milk. Nor is any man free from the temptations of the extremist's attitude: many a lonely and unnoticed soul would gladly exchange the seemingly empty years ahead for the great moments of a Romeo or a Hamlet. And what can we say of their choice except that it is not the choice of the sensible man? Secondly, we discover a just balance between the depths of the hero's suffering and the heights of his joys. That the hero's joys and sorrows are equalized by his capacity for feeling, which is the same for one as it is for the other, we cannot doubt, for how can the bitterness of the loss of a Juliet, or of a kingdom, or of power, or of reputation, or of life itself, be measured except by the sweetness of possession? How much it means to the hero to possess what he prizes, so much the loss—no more, no less. Thirdly, the power of poetry to shadow forth the universal suggests to us, as we follow the fortunes of the hero, that in a correct reckoning one man is neither better off nor worse off than another. The hero's change of fortune, universalized, suggests that good and evil, the fundamental modes of experience, imply one another so necessarily that no one may hope to escape from the grief which is the counterpart of his gladness.

And it is this power of poetry to universalize—to present a tragic hero as the representative of mankind—which finally lifts us, as we witness the rise and fall of a man like ourselves, above envy and pity, filling us with a sense of an all-prevailing justice which brings to every man equal measures of suffering and joy.

## IV

Aristotle's definition of tragedy epitomizes the virtues of his method and the weakness of his aim in the study of poetry. Since the definition appears in the *Poetics* near the beginning of the discussion of tragedy and is followed by generalizations which seem to depend upon its acceptance, an unwary reader might mistakenly infer that these generalizations are consequences deduced from supposedly self-evident assumptions. The answer to such a misunderstanding of the Aristotelian method is to be found in the difference between the order of investigation and the order of demonstration. In his investigation of tragedy, Aristotle started by analyzing the available specimens into their distinguishable parts, proceeded by generalizing concerning the constituent elements of tragedy, and ended by synthesizing his findings in the definition. In demonstrating his results, however, he reverses the steps of investigation: in the *Poetics* he starts with his definition, proceeds by discussing the generalizations which it summarizes, and ends by supporting each generalization with examples chosen from particular tragedies. Properly understood, then, the definition marks the end of the investigation of tragedy and the beginning of the demonstration of its nature. But although the definition is the culmination of an admirable scientific method, its ending in a puzzling metaphor signalizes the inadequacy of Aristotle's attempt to explain tragedy by treating it as though it were charged with feeling but lacking in meaning.

"Tragedy," says Aristotle, "is an imitation of an action that is serious, complete, and of adequate magnitude—in language embellished in different ways in different parts —in the form of action, not of narration—through pity and terror effecting the purgation of these emotions." Here we have the kind of logical definition, invented by Socrates and perfected by Aristotle, which first places the object to be defined in its proximate genus and then distinguishes it as a species by listing its specific differences. Like all other forms of poetry, tragedy is an imitation of an action: imitation is the genus to which tragedy, as one of the imitative arts, belongs. The action represented in a tragedy, however, has qualities which distinguish it from the actions represented in other arts and other kinds of poetry. It is serious, complete, and of adequate magnitude. A single incident of suffering or enjoying may serve as material for a lyric poem or a dramatic episode, but the action of a tragedy cannot be less than the series of incidents, in probable or necessary sequence, of a change of fortune. Unlike the little ups and downs of comedy, which can be laughable because they are trivial, the change of fortune of a tragedy is serious, with great and grave consequences; therefore, a tragedy loses effectiveness if its action is too brief to make a serious impression or too long for its incidents, which reveal the probability or necessity of the change of fortune, to be easily retained in memory. A (Greek) tragedy is composed of choral odes and dramatic episodes, and each of these is embellished in its own way, one with melody, the other with meter—a point which further distinguishes (Greek) tragedy from other kinds of (Greek) poetry. Tragedy is distinguished from epic and narrative poetry by its dramatic form: its main incidents are in the form of action taking place at the moment they are seen or read. And since (presumably) each kind of poetry is most clearly distinguished by the particular pleasure derived from its special emotional effects, a poem which meets the other tests may be positively identified as a tragedy by the pleasure it affords while purging us of the emotions of pity and terror.

Interest in Aristotle's definition has always centered on his concluding phrase—"through pity and terror effecting the purgation of these emotions"—on the famous metaphor which brings to an anticlimax a study which, had it been guided only by a scientific method, should have resulted in a clear, literal, and objective definition of tragedy. When we remember that Aristotle is necessarily defining only Greek tragedy in relation to Greek art and poetry, we must admit that the early parts of his definition possess the qualities of scientific description. The concluding phrase manifests, however, a sharp break with his method. From a consideration of those qualities of tragedy which may be objectively observed and analyzed, he turns suddenly to the effects of tragedy as they are subjectively experienced by the spectator. At the end of a series of generalizations, literally applicable to the individual tragedies from which they have been derived by induction, he falls back upon a metaphor suggested by the science and art of medicine.

Though it does not take us far, probably the only safe guide to the meaning of Aristotle's medical metaphor is the passage in the *Politics* in which he discusses the place of music in education. Many benefits, he tells us, are derived from music: some melodies are valuable aids in education; others offer relaxation and recreation after exertion; and still others offer a restoring and healing purgation to those who are troubled by an excess of such feelings as religious enthusiasm. This purgation, he goes on to say, is an important function of art; through catharsis those who are especially susceptible to pity, fear, and enthusiasm, and all others in a lesser degree of intensity, find a pleasurable relief. That is all we find in the passage, except the promise that he will provide a fuller explanation of catharsis in his study of poetry.

Since the *Poetics*, as we know it, fails to keep this promise, some scholars have assumed that the part of the text containing the explanation has been lost. Several considerations suggest reasonable doubts concerning this possibility. Although parts of the *Poetics* may be missing, is it likely that the most important part should be lost and completely forgotten? And since Aristotle's promised explanation of catharsis would necessarily trace this mysterious effect to its causes, making possible a consideration of the relative effectiveness of these causes as they appear in particular tragedies, is it likely that Aristotle had worked out an explanation of how pity and terror are pleasurably purged and yet failed to use it or to refer to it in any of the many scattered passages in which he discusses how these emotions are effectively excited? It seems more likely that Aristotle, realizing that an explanation would raise the question of the meaning of tragedy, decided that his metaphor was by itself sufficiently clear to serve its purpose.

Although a metaphor is anticlimactic at the end of a scientific investigation, Aristotle's theory of catharsis, as it is explained in the passage in the *Politics,* admirably suits his purposes in the study of poetry. It answers Plato's extreme criticisms of poets and poetry. Poetry, Plato had charged, feeds the passions, which should be starved. Poetry, Aristotle seems to reply, provides a healthful emotional outlet, a beneficial mean between the dangerous extremes of surrender to passion and suppression of feeling. The poets, Plato had charged, are untrustworthy teachers. The poets, Aristotle seems to reply, are to be judged, not as teachers, but as contributors to the emotional well-being of mankind. Indeed, the theory of catharsis is Aristotle's solution to the ancient quarrel between poetry and philosophy: the poet is granted an honored function in the realm of the feelings, but the philosopher remains king in the realm of meaning.

## Tragedy

If Aristotle's metaphor were altogether clear and illuminating, we might accept it as proof that philosophy and science must end, as they so often begin, in poetry. Instead of a clear and full illumination, however, it provides an intriguing and tantalizing partial illumination: in it we find the question to be answered rather than the answer to the question. This question presents an apparent paradox. The misfortunes of men like ourselves excite such unpleasant feelings as pity and terror, and yet the total effect of tragedy is pleasing. Aristotle recognizes this apparent paradox but fails to explain it. Although he discusses in detail the objective causes of the spectator's pity and terror, judging the suitability of heroes, of plots, and of the parts of plots by their effectiveness in exciting these emotions, he *nowhere* points out the cause or causes of the catharsis which supposedly transforms pity and terror into pleasure. His metaphor merely asserts that this transformation takes place; it contains no hint as to why it takes place. For this reason, scholars who accept Aristotle's metaphorical definition of tragedy are obliged to furnish their own explanations of its meaning, with the result that there are said to be now available more than sixty interpretations of the theory of catharsis.

The theory of catharsis, as Aristotle presents it, ignores the manifest intention of the Greek tragic poets to demonstrate the fundamental conditions of human destiny. Aeschylus, the inventor of tragedy, obviously regarded himself as a teacher of personal freedom and responsibility and his tragedies as striking illustrations of the divine justice which finally prevails in human affairs. Sophocles, by stressing the dignity and beauty of the heroic human spirit, taught a religious acceptance of ordained events, however terrible they may be. Euripides, the rebel and skeptic, was torn between a desire to equal the triumphs of his predecessors in demonstrating the justice of strange dooms and a desire to surpass them by using drama to expose the injustices of the *status quo* in society. Each poet developed a distinctive attitude or solution, but all aimed at the solution of one and the same problem, the problem of justice; and it would be ridiculous to say of any one of them that as an artist in tragedy his purpose was merely to play upon the emotions of the spectator or to afford the spectator a healthful but inexplicable pleasure.

Aristotle's preoccupation with the emotional effect of poetry obliged him to ignore the plain and obvious fact that every true tragedy is a demonstration of the justice of the unalterable conditions of human experience. If he had been willing to admit that the reason that tragedy leaves us at the end with a sense of reconciliation rather than with one of horror is that it affects both the mind and the feelings by presenting a view of life in which the idea of justice is central, he might have avoided his puzzling and unsatisfactory metaphor and concluded his definition with a clear, literal, and objective statement of its essential quality. "Tragedy," *he might then have said,* "is an imitation of an action that is serious, complete, and of adequate magnitude—in language embellished in different ways in different parts—in the form of action, not of narration"—*revealing a just relation between good and evil in the life of a representative man.*

# PART TWO

# On the Relation between
# Good and Evil

# III *

# The Tragic Meaning

# of *Moby Dick*

THE tragic spirit appeared in American literature first in the form of fiction rather than in the form of drama. Hawthorne and Melville never wrote for the theatre. Melville, the greater tragic artist of the two, did, however, under the good influence of *King Lear*, come as close to dramatic form as a novelist can. In *Moby Dick*—inspired by the success of Hawthorne's tragic *Scarlet Letter* and by his own need to describe life as it is rather than to please the romantic tastes of his public—Melville groped for a medium in which to tell the story of a representative man, for he now desired to draw a tragic and realistic picture of life.

*Tragedy*

## I

Some years before the middle of the last century one Captain Ahab of the *Pequod,* who had already given forty years to whaling, set out from Nantucket on what the owners, Captains Peleg and Bildad, expected to be a three years' whaling cruise. The owners thought highly of their captain, although Bildad phrased their opinion strangely in telling Ishmael, a new member of the crew, that he was lucky to serve under a moody good captain rather than under a laughing bad captain. Bildad told Ishmael a few other things about Ahab. His name, he said, was the ignorant whim of his crazy widowed mother, who had died before Ahab's first birthday. An old squaw at Gayhead had once said that the name would some day prove prophetic, but whether this was a prediction of the kingly nature of the man or of some deep capacity for evil no one knew. One thing was certain: Ahab's was the keenest and surest lance out of Nantucket, and the owners had every right to expect another profitable voyage for their ship.

But Bildad and Peleg were unaware of Ahab's true intentions. His mind was not on profit, and not even on the parting with his young wife, whom he had married three voyages back; it was on Moby Dick. On his last voyage he had crossed the path of the great white whale, then the terror of the seas, and lost a leg in the encounter. In the intensity of his suffering on the long passage home he had been a little out of his mind, and ever since he had given way to a desperate and savage moodiness. Peleg expected Ahab's dark passion to wear off at sea, but Peleg could not plumb the depths of Ahab's character.

## The Meaning of Moby Dick

Because Ishmael the wanderer sailed on the *Pequod's* last cruise and lived to tell the story, every reader of Melville's *Moby Dick* knows that Ahab sailed for vengeance. Possessed by one inflexible purpose—to destroy the white whale—he forgot both love of life and child and duty to his owners. Ishmael the wanderer became the spectator of a great drama of the sea. Day after day he witnessed the heroic madness of the captain. He took part in the final three-day chase of the white whale. By chance the only survivor of the crew, he floated about, until rescued by the *Rachel*, on the only bit of wreckage from the lost *Pequod*, Queequeg's coffin.

Through these memorable events every reader of Melville knows that the *Pequod* set out on an errand of vengeance, but few recall that to Captain Ahab the voyage was also a quest for certainty that ended in his great discovery. Ahab was not one to rest content with acting in events which he did not understand. He was determined not only to conquer the whale but also to understand the meaning of his conflict with the mighty beast. Before the *Pequod* set sail Peleg told Ishmael: "Ahab's above the common; Ahab's been in colleges, as well as 'mong the cannibals; been used to deeper wonders than the waves; fixed his fiery lance in mightier, stranger foes than whales." And so the madness of Ahab on the voyage was the madness of a man whose reason and imagination were keyed to their highest pitch, and the end of the chase was at one and the same time the foredoomed defeat of Ahab and the moment of his great discovery. In losing his life Ahab discovered its meaning.

## II

Although the full import of Ahab's discovery has seldom been grasped, it has a powerful effect on the reader. It invests the story with such significance that the reader feels *Moby Dick* to be something more than melodrama. As a record of the sensational events leading to the disastrous end of Ahab's vengeance, it is melodramatic, but as the revelation of the meaning of a man's character and fate, it becomes tragic.

The power of art brings us an awareness of meanings even when our comprehension nods. And since it is perfectly possible to feel that a work of art is great without knowing why, enthusiasm often precedes understanding in our judgment of a classic. The power of art reaches us through every door to experience, through the senses, the feelings, and the imagination; and although an intellectual order informs great writings, making them immediately acceptable to intelligent beings, the comprehension and abstract statement of this pattern is more often a consequence than a condition of appreciation. That conscious understanding is not necessary to feeling does not mean that we can long be satisfied to feel without knowing, for great power excites a natural curiosity concerning our feelings and their causes. The satisfaction of this curiosity would be a sufficient motive for a search into the meaning of *Moby Dick*.

Melville's classic of the sea failed to arouse even a feeling of its greatness in the public to which it was offered—for reasons which are probably related to its meaning. In the sixty years since Melville's death, however, some barrier between *Moby Dick* and the reader has weakened, and a wave of enthusiasm for the story of Ahab has swept the curious into a search for its meaning—a search which has taken a strange turn. Instead of seeking to explain the essential greatness of the book in terms of Ahab's vengeance and his apparent defeat, in terms of his quest for certainty and his great discovery, the critics of *Moby Dick* have become absorbed in mere *hidden* meanings, in the interpretation of vague symbols and the ferreting out of concealed analogies.

This curious effort on the part of critics to make each specific object of the book correspond to a suitable abstraction, this assumption that it is necessary to decode Melville's story in order to get at the meaning, had its beginnings in the notion that *Moby Dick* is an allegory. The well-known quotation from Melville's letter to Hawthorne seems to support this notion. Thanking Hawthorne for his letter in praise of *Moby Dick*, Melville wrote: "Why, ever since Adam, who has got to the meaning of this great allegory—the world? Then we pigmies must be content to have our paper allegories but ill comprehended." Unquestionably too much reliance has been placed on this quotation. Melville does not say that he has written an allegory in distinction from other books, which are not allegories; rather he speaks of the world and of books as allegories, a term which he may have chosen particularly because he is addressing Hawthorne. And if anyone feels that Melville meant explicitly to link himself with Hawthorne as a writer of allegories in the true sense of the word, how can he explain the passage in *Moby Dick* itself in which Melville expresses his fear that the ignorant may mistake the book for "a hideous and intolerable allegory"? As evidence, the specific statement in *Moby Dick* more than cancels the comment in the letter about books in general.

Yet *Moby Dick* is rich in overtones and subtleties which seem to justify a search for hidden meanings. As he wrote it, Melville brooded on the riddle of existence and doubtless thought of transposing actualities into the key of abstraction, the method which had absorbed Swedenborg and influenced Emerson, as one way to the solution. Part of the fascination of Ahab springs from the unswerving intentness with which he pursues both the whale and the meaning of his own life. He wills to be lord of the meaning of the event as well as of the event itself. "All visible objects, man," he says, "are but as pasteboard masks. But in each event—in the living act, the undoubted deed—there, some unknown but still reasoning thing puts forth the mouldings of its features from behind the unreasoning mask. If man will strike, strike through the mask!"

These subtleties should be understood primarily, however, in relation to the whole drama of Ahab. Because his quest for meaning goes on throughout the story, *Moby Dick* is filled with thwarted gleams of insight, with desperate searchings, with hints at symbols which, like the half-truths uttered by the characters in *King Lear*, are designed chiefly to turn the mind of the reader toward the profounder significance of the story itself. Melville is concerned to have the reader know that the story is the flesh and blood of life and not a collection of scarecrow garments chosen to conceal his own preconceived pattern of abstractions. Melville felt that whatever essential meaning lies in *Moby Dick* could be found in the life of a living Ahab by an Ahab himself. Further, the meaning goes far beyond abstract comprehension; it must come through the senses, the feelings, and the imagination, not merely through the understanding. For this reason *Moby Dick* is primarily a tragic interpretation of an action, not a philosophical essay, not a dance of symbolic phantoms. Ahab is a man and not a force, the sea is the sea and not a symbol, and the whale is a whale and not an arbitrary sign of evil. "So ignorant are most landsmen," says Melville, "of some of the plainest and most palpable wonders of the world, that without some hints touching the plain facts, historical and otherwise, of the fishery, they might scout at Moby-Dick as a monstrous fable, or still worse and more detestable, a hideous and intolerable allegory."

The growing fame of *Moby Dick* in the past fifty years has been based on its merits as a powerful story, as an action true to life as it is, not as Melville thought it ought to be. Its significance has seemed to lie in grasping life as a whole, in cutting cleanly to those centers of meaning which elude us in our own experience. As a dramatic story it has been compared with *King Lear.* The search for the meaning of *Moby Dick* ought first of all to be in keeping with this appreciation. Before we probe into hidden meanings, what is the meaning of Ahab's purpose and of his victory in defeat, of his quest and its reward in his discovery, the meaning involved in the powerful effect which Ahab's story has had on our senses, our feelings, and our imaginations?

### III

It is not unfair to say that critics would never have turned to hidden meanings if the significance of the story itself were sufficiently clear in their minds. Their error is pardonable. They have been confused first by the form of the story. With its heightened and impassioned language, its substitution of imaginative for homely details, its hardness relieved only by the pathos of little Pip, its revelation of the only great tragic hero of nineteenth-century American literature, its sense of necessity and finality, *Moby Dick* is like no other novel. It must be understood as drama, for in it Melville had arrived at the tragic view of life. And one understands its tragic import by understanding the story, by grasping the relation of the hero's character to his fate. Here, it seems to me, the critics have failed to follow the story through. They have stopped to brood with Ahab during the course of his quest and failed to go on with him to the discovery which throws light on all he had experienced. Curiously enough, Melville sought to drive home the importance of Ahab's discovery with the most striking bit of symbolism in the book, the incident of the sky hawk which goes down with the *Pequod;* and significantly, this is the one symbol for which the search for *hidden truth* has yet found no meaning.

The groping of Melville toward a medium of communication suited to his story is one lead toward its meaning. As a writer he began, as did other great Americans, with the urge for self-expression, the desire to record his own experiences. The pronounced individualism of American character, strengthened in some instances by the puritan habit of introspection, accounts for the beginnings of American literature in the personal narratives of Sewall, Woolman, and Edwards and for the promise of its high point in the journals of Emerson, Thoreau, and Melville.

To many of these writers self-expression was the end; to others it was the beginning of a search for an objective medium of communication. Young Melville, fortunate adventurer in the South Seas, had no need at first to go beyond the limits of self-expression. The record of his own experiences, unlike the journals of bookish young men, was immediately interesting to the public. Once he had been on the island of Nukuheva, he had only to tell his story; and Melville was the kind of storyteller who destroys the boundaries fixed between fact and fiction. The deserved success of *Typee* encouraged him to continue this method of telling his own story. In rapid succession appeared *Omoo, Mardi, Redburn,* and *White-Jacket;* in all these except perhaps *Mardi,* the fascination of the material, coupled with Melville's artistry, continued to make desirable public property out of private experiences.

But in *Moby Dick* Melville groped for a medium in which to tell the story of another, for he now had in mind an objective rather than a subjective picture of life. The result was partly still in the autobiographical and romantic manner familiar to the readers of his earlier tales, but partly also in the manner of great drama. In *Moby Dick* Melville and his romantic moods are still present in the form of Ishmael, but it is Ahab the actor, not Ishmael the narrator, who is the center of interest throughout. Just as Ishmael is forgotten in the awe excited by the central actor—the reader hardly notices his fall from the whaleboat and is startled when he reappears in the epilogue—so *Moby Dick* is in spirit a tragic drama rather than a romantic novel or a mere tale. In spite of the great amount of space devoted to the whale and to the sea, the reader never loses sight of the hero and his destiny.

The action itself has all the perfections which Aristotle finds in the best tragic plots. It is complex, and like that

of *Oedipus the King,* artfully combines the main change
of fortune with a discovery and a reversal of intention.
Oedipus, seeking to do good by finding the unknown murderer, brings about his own downfall by the discovery that
he is himself the guilty one. So Ahab, although he only
intensifies his grief by his attempt to destroy the cause of
evil, discovers the meaning of his fortunes in the end
which his vengeance brings upon him. The plot of *Oedipus
the King* is rich in minor reversals of intention. Whoever,
for example, seeks to evade one of the oracles succeeds
only in helping to fulfill it. *Moby Dick* also moves by
minor reversals of intention; one of the best leads to the
end. On the third day of the chase Ahab discovers that
he is now the pursued, not the pursuer. "Ay, ay, it must
be so. I've oversailed him. How, got the start? Ay, he's
chasing *me* now; not I, *him*—that's bad; I might have
known it, too."

The seething power of its action brings the story again
and again directly into dramatic form. Chapter 37 starts
significantly with a stage direction: "(*The cabin; by the
stern windows; Ahab sitting alone, and gazing out.*)" The
chapter itself consists of a single dramatic soliloquy by
Ahab. The next two chapters follow the same form with
Starbuck and Stubb as actors, and Chapter 40 brings the
harpooneers and sailors together in a little play. Chapter
108, a scene between Ahab and the carpenter, is entirely
in dramatic form, as are Chapters 120, 121, 122, 127, and
129. The first sentence of the epilogue clearly reveals Melville's attitude toward the spirit and form of his story:
"*The drama's done.*" The use of an epilogue is itself an
instance of the dramatic form of *Moby Dick.* In Chapter
33 Melville refers to himself as "the tragic dramatist who
would depict mortal indomitableness."

## *The Meaning of* Moby Dick

The difference between *Moby Dick* and *Typee,* Melville's first romantic novel, may be seen most clearly in the contrast between the ever-present sense of inevitability of the former and the endless uncertainty of the latter. The chief source of interest in *Typee* is suspense. The hero, wandering into a valley of the island of Nukuheva, does not know whether the valley is Typee or Happar, whether he will fall into the hands of good islanders or of cannibals. When, made helpless by an injury, he is discovered by the islanders, he does not know whether he is captured or befriended. The suspense continues through the long recital of the kindnesses and habits of the islanders; their every act may be either that of a good Samaritan or that of a cannibal caring for his food supply. And the possibilities are kept nicely balanced to the very end. The technique of *Moby Dick* is, in contrast, based not on suspense but on the problem of leading up to an inevitable end. Foreshadowing, the familiar device of tragic drama, helps mark the difference between *Typee,* the romantic tale of chance fortune and misfortune, and *Moby Dick,* the tragic revelation of the fixed conditions of human experience. The thousand little hints and signs and symbols are so many fingers pointing to what must come. Melville meant them to point to Ahab's discovery so that the reader may reflect on all that happens in its light; yet many searchers for hidden meanings have sought the answer in the pointers themselves.

## IV

What is the tragic meaning of *Moby Dick?* Had Melville been a philosopher instead of an artist, he might have written down and developed a series of propositions about human experience, but Melville was an artist in tragedy, not a philosopher. He gives us not propositions but the actions on which propositions are based, not the law but the hero whose fate is a revelation of the law.

Ahab, like all great heroes, is enough like other men to make his fate representative of their own: he is also unusual enough to hold the interest of his fellows. Intensity makes Ahab unusual and a hero. His outstanding characteristic is his unyielding will to do or die, his fierce intentness of purpose, from which no one, not even the gods, may swerve him. "Swerve me? ye cannot swerve me, else ye swerve yourselves! man has ye there. Swerve me? The path to my fixed purpose is laid with iron rails, whereon my soul is grooved to run."

The intensity of Ahab's purpose and its concentration on a single object, Moby Dick, make him a striking and dramatic example of the common fate of man. He is the extreme chosen to throw light on the mean.

And there is a Catskill eagle in some souls that can alike dive down into the blackest gorges, and soar out of them again and become invisible in the sunny spaces. And even if he forever flies within the gorge, that gorge is in the mountains; so that even in his lowest swoop the mountain eagle is still higher than other birds upon the plain, even though they soar.

Such an eagle is the soul of Ahab. He lives in the mountain gorges and sunny spaces of feeling; most men live on the plains.

Although Melville has made Ahab different in degree from other men, he has not made him different in kind. Ahab is no madman in the ordinary sense of the word. Melville calls him a monomaniac, but he clearly relishes the notion that Ahab's monomania is only more intense than the purposes of his fellows. Nor did Melville suppose that any gulf separated the whalers from ordinary people. Whaling was as much a part of the ordinary business of 1851 as one of the heavy industries, let us say, is a part of the life of today. To Melville the repeated actions of the whalers—the search, the pursuit, the kill, the trying of the oil, and the cleaning of the ship—seemed perfectly representative of life.

Oh! my friends, but this is man-killing! Yet this is life. For hardly have we mortals by long toilings extracted from this world's vast bulk its small but valuable sperm; and then, with weary patience, cleansed ourselves from its defilements, and learned to live here in clean tabernacles of the soul; hardly is this done, when—*There she blows!*—the ghost is spouted up, and away we sail to fight some other world, and go through young life's old routine again.

## V

Ahab is a striking representative of man by virtue of his degree of difference from others. His unfaltering resolution is the sure origin of dramatic action, the first essential of great poetry, and cannot fail to excite interest, respect, and even awe. He is equally suited to be the representative man by his universality. A canon of neoclassical criticism required that tragic heroes be kings or princes, so that their fall, involving others, might excite the greatest possible amount of sympathy and interest. Melville makes certain that his hero is known as a man of consequence. Ahab is the lord of his little universe, the *Pequod;* all his world must rise or fall with him, in seeking either profit or vengeance. "Among whale-wise people," says Melville, "it has often been argued whether, considering the paramount importance of his life to the success of the voyage, it is right for a whaling-captain to jeopardize that life in the active perils of the chase." Melville quickly supports the theory of Ahab's supremacy in the course of events. "Ahab seized a loaded musket from the rack (forming part of most South-Seamen's cabin furniture), and pointing it toward Starbuck, exclaimed: 'There is one God that is Lord over the earth, and one captain that is lord over the *Pequod.*—On deck!'" Starbuck, as fearless as Ahab himself, does not challenge the captain's authority.

Intensity is the key to the character of the hero in life and in drama. The simplest kind of hero is intense only in will; greater, more complex heroes add intensity of thought and feeling to mere intentness of will. Heroes of the simplest kind are commonest; the uncompromising will to win is at once evident in Lord Clive, in General Grant, in Wolfe at Quebec, in Marlowe's Tamburlaine. Only the rarest of heroes—a Lincoln in life or a Hamlet in drama—are as intense in thought and feeling as they are in will.

Ahab is raised above the level of a Tamburlaine by his desire to grasp the meaning of events. Throughout his pursuit of the whale he is tortured by the desire to foresee and understand. Like Macbeth, and like Ibsen's Solness, he turns, in the lack of a reasonable account of the natural, to the seemingly supernatural, hoping to find in the Parsee's prophecies a guarantee of victory. On Ahab's search for the significance of his own story depend the many hints, half-truths, and partly concealed meanings in *Moby Dick.* Because he has never pondered on the meaning of life, Tamburlaine at the end discovers only that the answer is "yes" to his question:

# The Meaning of Moby Dick

Shall sickness prove me now to be a man,
That have been termed the terror of the world?

Because his was a quest for certainty as well as a quest for vengeance, Ahab at the end discovers what it means to be a man.

Although we now recognize Captain Ahab as the most impressive tragic figure in nineteenth-century American literature, we cannot maintain that he is a perfect tragic hero. In an important respect he falls short of the ideal.

In his lack of range of feeling Ahab disappoints us as a hero. His capacity for feeling is tremendous, but his feelings are centered entirely on himself and his problem. We see only his passionate hatred of the whale: the spell which it casts over him is such that no consideration for another, no human sympathy, can penetrate. Because of their association on the *Pequod,* Starbuck is nearest to him in intensity and resolution. Ahab at times is almost capable of taking his point of view. "Starbuck," he says on the second day of the chase,

of late I've felt strangely moved to thee; ever since that hour we both saw—thou know'st what, in one another's eyes. But in this matter of the whale, be the front of thy face to me as the palm of this hand—a lipless, unfeatured blank. Ahab is forever Ahab, man.

"Ahab is forever Ahab"—character is permanent—and he rightly says that it is strange for him to be moved by feeling for another. Characteristically, he immediately drowns the alien feeling in the passion of his purpose.

Ahab's purpose was not only to kill the whale but also to understand the events which beat against his own live heart. For this reason his final victory, coming at the moment of the loss of his ship and his life, is a victory of insight as well as of will. His last words are of triumphant understanding, and he thinks first of the triumph of his understanding, only later of the triumph of his will.

Oh, now I feel my topmost greatness lies in my topmost grief. Ho, ho! from all your furthest bounds, pour ye now in, ye bold billows of my whole foregone life, and top this one piled comber of my death! Toward thee I roll, thou all-destroying but unconquering whale; to the last I grapple with thee; from hell's heart I stab at thee; for hate's sake I spit my last breath at thee.

So at last came the answer to Ahab's quest. The moment of insight in which he sees that his grief and his greatness are but the two sides of his nature, one impossible without the other, is Ahab's great discovery and the key to the tragic meaning of *Moby Dick*.

## VI

We should expect the remarkable bit of symbolism at the end of *Moby Dick* to derive its meaning from Ahab's discovery. And indeed with his discovery in mind there is no longer anything puzzling about the incident, which occurs at the moment of the sinking of the *Pequod:*

At that instant, a red arm and a hammer hovered backwardly uplifted in the open air, in the act of nailing the flag faster and yet faster to the subsiding spar. A sky-hawk that tauntingly had followed the main-truck downward from its natural home among the stars, pecking at the flag, and incommoding Tashtego there; this bird now chanced to intercept its broad fluttering wing between the hammer and the wood; and simultaneously feeling that ethereal thrill, the submerged savage beneath, in his death-gasp, kept his hammer frozen there; and so the bird of heaven, with archangelic shrieks, and his imperial beak thrust upward, and his whole captive form folded in the flag of Ahab, went down with his ship, which, like Satan, would not sink to hell till she had dragged a living part of heaven along with her, and helmeted herself with it.

By the symbolism of this improbable incident, the end of the *Pequod* is made to correspond precisely with the end of her master. Her flag is indeed the flag of Ahab's disposition. Just as he had carried his unconquerable spirit into defeat, so the *Pequod* carries a bit of heaven into the deeps. The end of Ahab is not unrelieved defeat, but victory in defeat; and the main point of *Moby Dick* is that any great human action will show that the heavens and the deeps, eternal symbols of man's triumphs and disasters, are merely the limits of his experience, related to each other through that experience and dependent upon each other and upon him for their meaning.

However right we may be as to the nature of Ahab's quest and the meaning of his discovery, are we justified in generalizing about life on the basis of his story? We know that Melville intended to create a work universally significant. And surely only a very limited mind could fail to agree with Ahab that man must be lord of the meaning of the event as well as of the event.

But the answer lies in Ahab. Even to the degree in which he differs from ordinary man, Ahab is well chosen as the representative man. He is neither saint nor sinner; and his madness is beyond common experience only in its intensity. His grand passion to do and to know makes evident human destiny on a scale larger than life. And all Melville's powers—his heightened language, his selec-

tion of significant details, his compression of the story—
enable the reader to feel and to see in the story all that
he would be likely to miss in the apparent chaos of life
itself.

Ahab, furthermore, is the captain, the leader of his
company; his fate is their fate; all that happens to him is
significant to others. But in the last analysis we can generalize from the story of one man only if some common
law governs the fortunes of all. *Moby Dick,* like all tragedies, stresses the inevitability with which fate flows from
character and by which the lot of the individual is governed by fixed conditions and not by chance. These conditions, if we judge by Ahab, are in human nature, chief
among them the principle whereby man is equal to himself. Ahab is the equal of Ahab. In the story this truth is
driven home by Starbuck before Ahab himself realizes it.
Knowing that Ahab is fully confident that neither man
nor god can turn him from his fixed purpose, Starbuck
warns him of the one spirit in the universe exactly equal
to his own. "Thou hast outraged, not insulted me, sir;
but for that I ask thee not to beware of Starbuck; thou
wouldst but laugh; but let Ahab beware of Ahab; beware
of thyself, old man." Starbuck's judgment is based on the
inner conflict in Ahab, which is balanced with a terrible
nicety throughout the chase. Not until his discovery does
Ahab realize the same truth. Then, in the feeling that
his greatness lies in his grief, he discovers that the only
compensations for his fate are to be found in himself,
the nature that is capable of an exaltation exactly equal to
his grief. Aside from the social irresponsibility of his acts
Ahab, who is different from other men in the degree of
his intensity, is like all other men in that he is equal to

himself. Ahab's victory equals his defeat, his joy equals his sorrow.

## VII

In spite of the success of his earlier books, Melville's tragic masterpiece was a complete failure with the public. Why? The answer is, I think, that in the 1850's the American people were almost all romantic optimists; they agreed with Rousseau that man is naturally good, and that only by institutions is he made bad, and they believed further that by reforming institutions they would in the not distant future build a world in which all would find complete happiness. Some of them were extreme utopians, each with his favorite panacea for human woes. They held conventions to exchange remedies, founded little experimental communities to try out their theories, and started, it must be admitted, the great reform movements of the nineteenth century. The great illusion of the age was that it is possible to kill the white whale of evil; and under the spell of this illusion, people could neither accept the story of a man who was himself destroyed in his efforts to destroy evil as a realistic picture of life, nor find satisfaction or a sense of reconciliation in Ahab's final discovery that all his woes, including the agony of his final defeat, were the price that he had to pay for the greatness of his unconquerable spirit.

One can imagine the kind of hero and plot that would have pleased the optimistic public of Melville's time. Ahab, a worthy sea captain, who has been badly wounded on a previous voyage by Moby Dick, a whale which has been running off with harpoons, smashing boats, and diminishing profits, says good-by to his wife and child, and with the full co-operation of his public-spirited owners, sets sail to free the seas of this menace to prosperity. After a long voyage, filled with suspense and excitement, he catches up with Moby Dick, kills him, and gets out of the carcass an unusually large amount of whale oil. He returns in triumph, is greeted at the dock by wife and child, owners, and citizens, and is elected president of the Whalers Benevolent Association.

Such a book would not only have pleased Melville's public; it would have seemed true to life and realistic to them, because it would have supported their favorite illusions, just as many modern books are thought to be profound and realistic because they support the favorite illusions of some of our contemporaries.

It may be fairly asked, if the American public of the 1850's could not accept tragedy as a true picture of life, why did they accept and applaud Hawthorne's *Scarlet Letter,* published only a year and a half before, in 1850? The answer, I think, is that the scene of *The Scarlet Letter* is laid in the past, in seventeenth-century colonial, Calvinistic, theocratic New England. The progressive, republican, romantic, and occasionally utopian American of 1850 could believe that tragedy is a true picture of life as it was in those far-off and benighted days, and could enjoy Hawthorne's wonderful story, without disturbing his illusions. But in 1851, Melville was writing about the present, about Ahab, a supposedly representative contemporary, and about the whaling industry, which was then as up-to-date a subject as the steel mills and airplane factories would be today. When the public of 1851 was asked to choose between its illusions and a tragic view of life, it chose to ignore Melville.

## *The Meaning of* Moby Dick

Of course, *Moby Dick* had from the beginning a small number of admirers, who kept it alive, even while Melville was completely forgotten by the general public. But why is *Moby Dick* now regarded as one of the great American books, why is Melville esteemed as one of the major American writers, not because of his earlier popular books, though they are indeed excellent of their kind, but because of the very books—*Moby Dick, Pierre,* and *Billy Budd*—which were either ignored or disliked at the time of their appearance?

One answer might be that now, for us, the scene of *Moby Dick,* like the scene of *The Scarlet Letter,* is laid in the past. The whaling fleet, its relics embalmed in a few New England museums, is now chiefly a romantic memory, and Captain Ahab, once a disturbing contemporary, seems to all save those who have a good memory for dates as far away in time as Hawthorne's Chillingworth, Dimmesdale, and Hester Prynne.

A much better answer is that, shaken by the events of the past forty years, and by the shadow of possible coming events, by two World Wars and by the possibility of a third, modern man, slowly and much against his will, is being deprived of the illusion that he can kill the white whale of evil and build a world in which grief is no longer the price of gladness.

# IV *

# Whitman's Consistency

IF WE ask what is the essential meaning of American literature from 1835 to 1865, we will find it in a tragic sense of the common destiny of men. This is surely the key by which we unlock the best in Emerson, Thoreau, Melville, and Whitman; and by this best we determine the shortcomings and the strength of Poe and Hawthorne. What the first of these men were in literature, they were in life; they felt themselves united with other men. Poe and Hawthorne, on the other hand, made the best they could of isolation, Poe defiantly, Hawthorne unhappily. This, I think, is the key to the meaning of American literature. It is related to world literature through its tragic sense of life; it is American because it links the doctrine of human equality to the notion of a common fate. This

78

satisfies the old question—what is American about American literature?—as no other answer does.

In writing of man's relation to humanity and to the universe, Whitman became the foremost American poet and a major figure in world literature. No other poet has been so true to American democracy, both to the variety and richness of the surface of American life and to the inner unity and universality of American ideals. No poet excels him in depth of feeling or in the ability, shown in his best passages, to communicate feeling by the use of words; in his ability to express human feelings, from the tenderness which we conventionally think of as feminine to the tragic and heroic feelings which we conventionally think of as masculine, Whitman is fully the equal of Sophocles and Shakespeare.

I

Whitman's method of communicating his world is that of giving selected pictures from his own experience. In this method he has the greatest confidence; although he speaks again and again of "the same old law" which he finds in his own experience, the thought of systematically formulating this law never occurs to him. He furnishes us with the materials; we must see the law as he has seen it, feel it as he has felt it. As he tells us in the preface to *November Boughs* (1888), his purposes were always implicit rather than explicit. "After completing my poems," he says, "I am curious to review them in the light of their own (at the time unconscious, or mostly unconscious) intentions, with certain unfoldings of the thirty years they seek to embody." And as we read the two important prefaces to his poems (of 1855 and 1888), we realize that these purposes never became explicit in his mind, that he could never formulate them systematically. For this he had no gift; when he tries to tell us in prose what his purposes are, he is apt to overlook the significance of his own verses: his attempt at explanatory prose simply becomes more poetry, as is evident from the ease with which he recast the 1855 preface into three new poems a year later.

In 1855, indeed, he was able to sum up his notion of the function of the poet, although he was unable to develop his statement sufficiently to make it clear. "Of all mankind," he wrote, "the great poet is the equable man. Not in him but off from him things are grotesque or eccentric or fail of their sanity. Nothing out of its place is good and nothing in its place is bad. He bestows on every object or quality its fit proportions neither more nor less." This, which might pass for an expression of democracy or mere indolence, rightly understood is not far from the genius attributed to Sophocles, "who saw life steadily and saw it whole." The right interpretation of this conception of the great poet's function shows us something far different from a desire to bask in perceptual sunshine; we detect a yearning to get beyond the evaluations of finite existence and to apprehend the perfection of everything in its place. For who has come closer to Spinoza's *intellectualis amor Dei* than has Whitman in the 1855 preface? "The known universe," he says, "has one complete lover and that is the greatest poet. He consumes an eternal passion and is indifferent which chance happens and which possible contingency of fortune or misfortune and persuades daily and hourly his delicious pay."

## II

From his poetry we judge that Whitman was unusually sensitive to the aesthetic surface of the world. He celebrated the infinite variety of phenomena and stressed the individuality of shapes, sounds, colors, and beings which attaches to the objects of aesthetic intuition. His poems are reminiscences of the rich texture of experience, duplications, as far as words can duplicate objects, of the content of his own consciousness. His appreciation of aesthetic surface was indeed so widely distributed that we find in his work a general vigor of recollection rather than the hypersensitivity to a limited kind of experience and the accompanying heightening of natural effects that may be found, for example, in Hawthorne or Poe. For this reason, perhaps, Whitman has been excelled, at one time or another, in nearly all the poetic modes which mimic the natural pageantry of consciousness. Discrimination and selection are necessary to this kind of work; the span of a single life is not sufficient to permit an adequate record of its own experience. Many passages of Whitman's record have the flatness of an inventory or official report; the names of objects of consciousness are filed, but they do not fill the consciousness of the reader.

If, then, Whitman's poems had been merely mementoes or copies of aesthetic surfaces, we should be less able to excuse the occasional lapses and technical shortcomings which we profitably overlook in considering his larger significance as a poet. An appreciation of phenomena was Whitman's natural endowment; his disdain for dressing and polishing limited surfaces sprang from his acquired conviction that the inner aspect of reality is more important to the poet. For him the poet is more than a craftsman, more than an artist in the materials of the surface; the poet is a seer whose vision is always of the outer phenomena in terms of the inner principles.

It is impossible to grasp fully Whitman's conception of the prophetic function of the poet without a glance at the background and origin of his method. Literary transcendentalism, from which Whitman's method derives, was one of those unforeseen consequences which enliven the history of thought. Based indirectly on certain conclusions of Kant, it profited by the surprisingly happy result of adding one error to another. Philosophy was not, as Kant thought, to be forever discomfited by an incomprehensible thing-in-itself, and poetry was not, as the transcendentalists thought, to remain as the only possible interpreter of the meaning of good and evil for human beings; yet the combination of these two erroneous conclusions gave impetus to a spiritual renaissance in poetry. The temperaments, even the abilities, of the literary transcendentalists were such that they could neither fully understand nor criticize the grammatically and logically tortuous passages of Kant's *Kritik;* nevertheless, they felt themselves aided and justified by his work, for its result was welcomed even by those unable to follow the premises leading up to it. The dogmatic rationalism of a period had foundered on problems that were for the time unanswerable. Only one conclusion could be drawn from this result, and the transcendentalists did not fail to draw it. The meaning and value of life are beyond the methods of rational, logical, and scientific procedure; hence where rational method and discipline have failed, poetic insight and imagination are once more free to assert their supremacy. In the fifty years following Kant's death in 1804 this conclusion spread like a rumor over the literary world on both sides of the Atlantic; Goethe, Wordsworth, Shelley, Emerson, and Whitman were among those who planned to take over the functions of a bankrupt philosophy in the name of poetry and imaginative thought.

It is apparent, therefore, that in approaching these men the critic needs both the feeling of the poet and the analytic ability of the philosopher. This is particularly true in respect to Whitman, for, unlike the others, he was born as a writer into this atmosphere. He takes the conclusions of the transcendentalists for granted, and, as a consequence, of all American writers he is least aware, in the matter-of-fact sense, of what he is doing. Whitman never perfected a special apparatus for thinking, as philosophers do, never troubled to distill the formulas and propositions of pure reason from the wine of experience, and since he did not himself experience moments either of pure feeling or of pure thought, his writings are not conveniently classified for the reader. They contain no purely intellectualized or expository passages, for in Whitman every feeling is a thought and every thought a feeling, just as every percept is a concept and every concept a percept. He generalized everything that he saw and specified everything that he thought; moreover, whatever he knew, he felt: his abstractions shine through concrete objects and are colored with emotion. This mode of cognition, though not illogical, is quite outside the scope of commonplace logic and scientific procedure. It is intuitional but not incommunicable, and it represents a return to the earliest modes of thought, a movement away from the poet of pure poetry, the philosopher of pure reason, the scientist of controlled and impersonal experiment. Whitman does more than keep his eye on the object; he makes the object a part of himself. Hence the essence of his method lies in the rejection of formulas in favor of the better, truer, more illuminating intuition derived from the full content of experience itself, in the rejection of abstractions in favor of concrete and living experience. Let me, Whitman might have said, not reason coldly as the philosopher, not feel blindly as the conventional poet, not experiment without reason or feeling as the small scientist; let me experience all things as a man, wholly and without limitation. Such an unlimited man is his ideal poet, and such unlimited experience is his goal in poetry. Whoever requires an intellectual account of what Whitman accomplished must be able to separate the pure elements of his work without losing sight of their necessary interdependence.

His elevated poetry invites interpretation, for who would read the poetry of prophecy and revelation without trying to know what is prophesied and revealed? In the face of Whitman's mysticism, which found expression in the years 1855–1856 in the outlines of the spiritual democracy governed by the two principles of the infinitude and equality of individuals,[1] we are curious to determine to what extent the poet's vision has reconciled the contradictions apparent in the phenomena of existence. We demand from Whitman the prophet, who insisted that his vision must influence social and political life, a consistency which is not required of the pure mystic. A sane consistency, not the foolish consistency which Emerson scorned, is a fair

---

[1] H. A. Myers, "Whitman's Conception of the Spiritual Democracy, 1855–1856," *American Literature,* November, 1934.

test for prophetic poetry; otherwise its pretensions are invalid. Even Emerson recognized the demands made by such consistency upon the results of intuition. "I cannot myself," he said, "use that systematic form which is reckoned essential in treating the science of the mind. But if one can say so without arrogance, I might suggest that he who contents himself with dotting a fragmentary curve, recording only what facts he has observed, without attempting to arrange them within one outline, follows a system also." *Leaves of Grass* dots such a "fragmentary curve." Whitman's experience was large; as he said, he contained multitudes, and did not fear an occasional contradiction. Yet we doubt not that his composure rested upon the certainty of his own consistency, upon his faith in the principles which at all important points integrated his experience.

### III

These principles of the inner world brought him into touch first with the problem of good and evil. The turmoil and coverings of the surface world, the inequalities manifest everywhere, are founded on an apparent hierarchy of values. One thing, we think, is better than another, another thing is still better, and so on ad infinitum. Whitman denies the inner reality of this apparent hierarchy; he limits the terms good and evil to the judgment of the surface world and reserves the term perfect for the inner quality of things.

How perfect the earth, and the minutest thing upon it!
What is called good is perfect, and what is called bad is just
    as perfect.

## Tragedy

This vision of things as they are under the surface, of real and perfect things, will not be obscured by any judgment of values. Is the judgment one of moral value?

> I am not the poet of goodness only, I do not decline to be
> the poet of wickedness also.

Nor will it be hidden by the illusion that some things are always good for the practical purposes of the individual. Nothing is intrinsically good, but all things are intrinsically perfect. Victory, viewed from the side of the inner meaning of life, is no more real, no better, than defeat.

> Have you heard that it was good to gain the day?
> I also say it is good to fall, battles are lost in the same spirit
> in which they are won.

Even the object judged of supreme value by people—the object contained between their hats and boots, life itself—cannot stand as good and good only in the light of the inner meaning of life, for in that light death is good also.

> Has any one supposed it lucky to be born?
> I hasten to inform him or her it is just as lucky to die, and
> I know it.

This attitude toward good and evil, first expressed in the 1855 preface, continues to the end. In the preface he says (speaking of the function of the poet): "If peace is the routine out of him speaks the spirit of peace, large, rich, thrifty, building vast and populous cities, encouraging agriculture and the arts and commerce—lighting the study of man, the soul, immortality—federal, state or municipal government, marriage, health, free trade, inter-travel by land and sea. . . . In war he is the most deadly force of the war. Who recruits him recruits horse and foot." If Whitman had been merely the poet of political democracy, of social betterment, and of optimistic humanitarianism, he would have condemned war and pitied its victims as unequal in their fate to the citizens of peace, but as the poet of the spiritual democracy, he is the poet of war as well as of peace, for neither war nor peace can disturb the eternal law of the world. As we see by later poems, his attitude toward war never changed.

> I saw battle-corpses, myriads of them,
> And the white skeletons of young men, I saw them,
> I saw the debris and debris of all the slain soldiers of the
> war,
> But I saw they were not as was thought,
> They themselves were fully at rest, they suffer'd not.

Even intimate contact with a surface turmoil as tremendous as the Civil War could not shake his faith in the inner world; after the event his attitude was precisely what it had been years before the rise and fall of the Confederacy.

Whitman consistently regarded good and evil as elements in experience rather than as intrinsic qualities of objects. Objects per se he regarded as perfect; good and evil he regarded as necessary elements in the experience of every individual. Hence he never declined to be the poet of evil as well as of good. Late in life, when a clergyman's "rounded catalogue divine complete" seemed to him to include only the aesthetic things, he compiled a supplementary list:

> The devilish and the dark, the dying and diseas'd,
> The countless (nineteen-twentieths) low and evil, crude
> and savage,
> The crazed, prisoners in jail, the horrible, rank, malignant,

## Tragedy

Venom and filth, serpents, the ravenous sharks, liars, the
    dissolute;
(What is the part the wicked and the loathsome bear within
    earth's orbic scheme?)
Newts, crawling things in slime and mud, poisons,
The barren soil, the evil men, the slag and hideous rot.

Whitman has often been called an optimist, but there is
certainly some loose use of terminology on the part of
those who have done so. In order to clarify terms, first it
is necessary to distinguish between the feeling of a moment, a brief mood such as is expressed in a lyric poem,
and the fairly consistent attitude of a lifetime, for it is the
possession of a consistent attitude that often distinguishes
the major poet from the minor. Second, it is important to
keep in mind that optimism cannot mean other than that
the amount of good in the world outweighs the amount of
evil, and that the amount of good increases as time goes
on, just as, on the other hand, pessimism must mean that
the amount of evil in the world outweighs the good, and
that the amount of evil increases as time goes on. By the
very nature of the terms there are only three possible consistent attitudes toward the problem of good and evil:
optimism, pessimism, and a third, the mean between the
extremes, the belief, namely, that good and evil are both
necessary aspects of experience, that one implies the other,
and that the quantities of both, roughly speaking, remain
and will remain in a state of balance. Only the great maintain a consistent attitude toward the problem: among consistent optimists may be numbered the philosopher Her-
bert Spencer and probably the poets Tennyson and
Browning; among consistent pessimists, the philosopher
Schopenhauer and the poet Leopardi; among adherents of

the third point of view, Heraclitus, Emerson ("Compensation"), Sophocles, Shakespeare, and all tragic poets, and Whitman himself. The reader of Whitman cannot miss the heroic and tragic quality of his verse, a quality which such composers as Gustav Holtz have caught in setting the words to music. This kinship of Whitman to the tragic comes from his fixed attitude toward good and evil, which is in harmony with that of the tragic poets. In "Song of Myself," in the elegies, in all his great poems, Whitman consistently maintained this essentially tragic and heroic attitude toward good and evil.

In several short lyrics (mostly late poems) he departed from this middle path. Once, for example, he set forth the doctrine of optimism definitively.

Roaming in thought over the Universe, I saw the little that
    is Good steadily hastening towards immortality,
And the vast all that is call'd Evil I saw hastening to merge
    itself and become lost and dead.

But this departure (1881) from his conception of good and evil as equally necessary elements in experience has the significant subtitle, "After Reading Hegel," suggesting a sequence of events which leads us to mistrust Whitman's vision on this occasion.

Aside from the doubtful evidence of this brief and late outburst, the presumption of Whitman's optimism rests on the misapprehension that his poetry consists in a vision of the America of the future. One necessarily falls with the other, for to understand his mystical vision of the spiritual democracy is to see what he himself must have felt, namely, that the eternal equality of individuals is a myth if some individuals experience less evil or more good than others. Nowhere else in his poetry did he see good increasing and evil diminishing. Suffering and grief touched him immeasurably, yet he never doubted that the object of his pity had shared the common lot. Envy he apparently did not experience. First and last he held to the view, consistent with the principles of the inner world, that good and evil are necessary and supplementary modes of experience, the same view that the tragic poet expresses in the inevitable change of fortune. Infinite tenderness against the background of a heroic and unshakable faith in the common lot of mankind in respect to good and evil furnishes the distinctive quality of much of his poetry.

If in an occasional short, lyrical outburst he departed from his lifelong attitude toward evil, preaching optimism, he as often yielded to moods of depression. "I Sit and Look Out" (1860) is a fair example.

> I sit and look out upon all the sorrows of the world, and
>     upon all oppression and shame. . . .
> All these—all the meanness and agony without end I sitting
>     look out upon,
> See, hear, and am silent.

Surely, judging by the relation of these exceptions to the main body of Whitman's work and by the fact that they contradict and negate one another, we must take them for what they are, the expression of the poet's moods rather than of his convictions, the evidence of how even as steadfast a spirit as Whitman wavers momentarily to the one side or the other of his set course. Needless to say, Sophocles and Shakespeare departed as often in mood from their general tragic attitude toward the world.

## IV

Important as the general problem of good and evil is to Whitman's position, the problem of death becomes peculiarly his own. How can he reconcile death with the equality of infinite individuals; is it not apparent on the surface that while some men die in the fullness of time, others die too young, and still others die too old? This problem attracted his attention at the very beginning; he had carefully considered death long before the Civil War.

> Has Life much purport?—Ah, Death has the greatest purport.

He had come to feel as early as 1855, or earlier, that the infinite personality includes death as well as life within its *present* experience. He reached this conclusion in the first poem, "Song of Myself"; in the following year he felt that we need not regret the loss of the young man who loses his life in the pursuit of life, for only he has learned the lesson of life

> Who favors body and soul the same,
> Who perceives the indirect assuredly following the direct,
> Who in his spirit in any emergency whatever neither hurries nor avoids death.

Three years later the boy in "Out of the Cradle Endlessly Rocking" pleads with the bird of lamentations for a clue to the meaning of life.

> Whereto answering, the sea,
> Delaying not, hurrying not,
> Whisper'd me through the night, and very plainly before daybreak,

### Tragedy

Lisp'd to me the low and delicious word death,
And again death, death, death, death.

His own songs "awaked from that hour" with the burden
that the meaning of life is death. Death he again affirmed
in the "Death Carol" of 1865. Experience in the hospitals
and on the battlefields confirmed his earlier faith; and the
death of his hero, Lincoln, inspired "When Lilacs Last in
the Dooryard Bloom'd," an elegy identical in essence with
the earlier "Out of the Cradle Endlessly Rocking."

Whitman's attitude toward death is difficult to explain
in intellectual terms, for here his mysticism is in the foreground. As far as it may be treated intellectually, there
are three possible interpretations, of which the third is the
most probable. The first is that Whitman, who again and
again affirmed immortality, upheld the common Christian
doctrine. But this seems improbable, for his system has no
place for the afterworld of rewards and punishments
which Emerson had already rejected.

And the threat of what is call'd hell is little or nothing to
me,
And the lure of what is call'd heaven is little or nothing to
me.

It is more likely that he sought to attach a new meaning to
immortality. Once his panpsychism led him to entertain
the possibilities of eternal birth.

And as to you Life I reckon you are the leavings of many
deaths,
(No doubt I have died myself ten thousand times before.)

In "Song of Myself" and elsewhere he was fascinated by
the eternity of matter, by the possibility that he would

92

lurk somewhere in the grass beneath the feet of generations to come. His mysticism led him to the thought that life is outer, phenomenal, illusory, and death, inner and real. He embodied a favorite metaphor in "Night on the Prairies" (1860) and again in abbreviated form in "Pensive and Faltering" (1868): as the day reveals one globe only, the night many, so death has much more to reveal than has life; the dead are living, and the living are specters.

Very early he saw, however, that the true significance of death lies in what it means as a *present* experience to the living rather than in the possibility of life after death. He felt the strange paradox that he who lives is always dying.

> O living always, always dying!
> O the burials of me past and present.

While we live we experience life, but we also experience death, which is a background giving meaning and depth to life. Life and death are opposites of the surface which are in some mysterious way reconciled in the depths of the soul's reality.

Beyond this it is impossible to present Whitman's treatment of death in intellectual terms, for this treatment, designed to counteract unreasoning fear and horror, addresses itself to the senses and feelings, to the heart and not to the mind. Such are the intention and effect of "Out of the Cradle Endlessly Rocking" and of "When Lilacs Last in the Dooryard Bloom'd," as every reader knows.

## V

From the treatment of good and evil and of life and death we learn how to grasp the largest categories implicit in Whitman's experience, the inner and outer aspects of reality. The locus of the spiritual democracy, the basis for tragic justice, is not in some far-off Platonic world of ideas or shadowy realm of essences; it is immanent in the experience of the individual. Nor is the inner world more real than the outer; it may be more important for the poet, for it is his special function to interpret it; the goal of the individual, however, is to live harmoniously according to the inner significance of experience and the outer pressure of circumstance. Even the poet is not content with piercing the outer turmoils and coverings of life to its inner significance. Whitman was concerned with the general problem of evil and also with the specific evils in American social life. Facing these problems squarely, he did not attempt to construct a compensatory spiritual world. Whitman's inner world is not an asylum, a refuge from the evils of the surface; it is a propaedeutic to action. The outer world is neither predominantly good nor predominantly evil; as experience, it is both good and evil; and the inner world, instead of leading us away from it, turns us, filled with a realization of eternal justice and fortified with a new courage and dignity, again toward social and political problems.

The experience of the individual is such that each of its two important aspects, the inner and the outer, throws light upon the other. In the eternal search for political and social justice the poet finds the clue to the inner justice of life. His mysticism, his vision of the inner life, follows the native forms and patterns of the surface of the world; the emphasis placed upon the worth of the individual and upon the equality of individuals in Whitman's political and social background becomes the spiritual principles of the infinitude and equality of individuals. In turn the surface world is to accept as ideals in the limited fields of social, political, and economic action the justice and equality eternally manifest in inner experience.

Whitman's democracy of the spirit arose from a desire to solve the problems of the surface world rather than from an impulse to avoid them; and the goal of his work is reached only when the two worlds are seen inseparably joined together. For this reason it is only from Whitman the prophet that we learn his lesson complete. As a prophet, Whitman was not a soothsayer; he did not attempt the miracle of foretelling the future except in the sense that one who grasps eternal laws understands also how they will work themselves out in time. With this last point he was much concerned; he united at all times intense patriotic fervor with his vision of eternal verities. His discovery of the eternal principles of the infinitude and equality of individuals strengthened his belief that the greatness of America lies in her surface resolve to glorify the individual and in her choice of equality as a surface ideal, just as his original faith in America, tempered by doubt and uncertainty, had led him to a vision of first principles. For these reasons, although he had his moments as patriot bard and others as pure mystic, it is only in the role of the prophet who interprets the world of the surface in terms of eternal laws that we fully understand Whitman and his work.

In the last analysis Whitman is consistent because the fragmentary curve which he dots is nothing more than the experience of the individual, in whom all opposites are reconciled. Good and evil as qualities of objects raise interminable problems, but they may be consistently explained as elements in the experience of the individual.

Death, a mysterious state when it is regarded as a future state of being, is intelligible when it is understood to be an ever-present background of the meaning of life. Finally, the individual can appreciate his own depths only when he realizes that his own infinitude and equality remain throughout the ceaseless change of circumstance.

> Out of politics, triumphs, battles, life, what at last finally remains?
> When shows break up what but One's-Self is sure?

Hence it is no reflection upon Whitman to say that he was from first to last a thoroughgoing and consistent individualist; there could be a reflection only if the individual were something opposed to the cosmic order, something opposed to the true state. Such a being, contained between his hat and his boots, has nothing in common with Whitman's simple separate person, for to Whitman the infinite universe is nothing more than the infinite possibilities of the individual's experience, and the true state, to paraphrase Emerson, is only the blended shadows of individuals.

A rare and fortunate combination of events furnished a method admirably suited to the forms of thought likely to arise from Whitman's social and political background. At the very time when a poet arose to celebrate a state which had its inception in "great persons," a state determined to treat only with individuals, transcendentalism had swung literary method out of the path of impersonal sciences and philosophies, finding in persons rather than in systems the source of its material. The intellectual movement from Kant through Emerson was half the preparation necessary to the appearance of Whitman;

the trend in political theory from Locke through Jefferson, and its exemplification, was the other half. All events conspired to further the celebration of the individual in prophetic poetry.

After Whitman there is not likely to be a philosophy native to America which is not touched by his imaginative insight. Yet Whitman himself is no metaphysician; his faith is poetic faith and not the conviction that follows logical demonstration; and analysis of his work leads us to the value of the sensuous content of his poetry as well as to the value of its abstracted philosophy. His methods sometimes run parallel to the methods of philosophy, but they are not the same. The cornerstones of his system must often rest on foundations which no logical system could recognize; and the faith of the reader in the community of infinite and equal persons, as Whitman conceives it, must ultimately rest on the power of his poetry.

# V ⁎

# *Macbeth* and *The Iceman Cometh:* Equivalence and Ambivalence in Tragedy

WHILE in England I was invited to speak on the opening day of the season at the Shakespeare Memorial Theatre on the subject of American drama. Although I was delighted to receive the invitation, I confess I had some misgivings about an assignment which seemed something like carrying coals to Newcastle and even more like carrying the spirit of the frontier to one of the cradles of civilization. As the day approached, I began to fear that my talk might be at best an irrelevant distraction and at worst an effrontery which could only be worse if it were given a little later in the season—on Shakespeare's birthday. I decided that a prudent man, in view of these possibilities, would not fail to find a place for Shakespeare in the story of American drama.

I began, therefore, by pointing out that what was perhaps the first theatre in America was built in Williamsburg, Virginia, in 1716, exactly one hundred years after the death of Shakespeare in 1616, and that the date of the first production of a play by Eugene O'Neill, the first American to win international fame as a dramatist, was 1916, exactly three hundred years after the death of Shakespeare. Since I could find nothing of importance in the American theatre on the two-hundredth anniversary of Shakespeare's death, I remarked that, for the sake of a clearer and more interesting history of our drama, the fathers of the Republic might well have chosen 1816 rather than 1776 for the Declaration of Independence.

My fears were groundless. The people I met at Stratford were genuinely interested in American drama, and it was not necessary for me to make Shakespeare central in its history or to end on the story of the American, Josephine Preston Peabody, who in 1910 won the Stratford Prize Competition with a verse drama, *The Piper*, which was presented in the Shakespeare Memorial Theatre on July 26 of that year. Nevertheless, to make clear my estimate of the achievement of O'Neill, our foremost tragic dramatist, I found it necessary to end with a reference to Shakespeare which I have now expanded.

## I

O'Neill, I said at Stratford, in his later plays seems to identify ambivalence with the tragic predicament of modern man, who is simultaneously attracted toward and repelled from objects, persons, actions, and even life itself; Shakespeare identifies the tragic predicament of man in all times and places with equivalence, with the two-sided nature of human feelings, whereby the source of our pleasure and joy is also so inevitably the source of anxiety and grief that man, in accordance with his capacity for feeling, which is always the same for joy as it is for sorrow, is fated to enjoy and suffer in equal measures. O'Neill may be said to have shown, perhaps better than any other modern dramatist, the sickness of an age and an aspect of tragedy peculiarly noticeable in our times; Shakespeare has shown, better than any other tragic dramatist, the equivalence of joy and sorrow, of guilt and remorse, which guarantees the justice of human destiny. Truly, "He was not of an age, but for all time."

*The Iceman Cometh* contains O'Neill's most explicit identification of ambivalence with the tragic predicament of modern man. As a few examples will show, the stories of the central figures in the play are variations of a single theme.

Harry Hope, proprietor of a run-down saloon, has not been out of it since the death of his wife twenty years before. He clings to the illusion that he loved his wife dearly and that her death was a loss without gain, but actually he hated her for nagging.

Theodore Hickman, known as Hickey, a successful salesman, always shows up for a spree at the time of Hope's birthday. Hickey, we discover late in the play, has murdered his wife. He believes at first that he has killed her because he loved her. Realizing that he can never live up to her patient and unwavering faith that he will some day give up drinking and bad company, he has, as he sees it, acted to save her from the crushing blows of repeated disappointments. He is forced by events, however, to recognize another side to his story: he loved her, but he also hated her. A born salesman, who loved his work and its possible diversions with free and easy companions, Hickey found in his wife's persistence in upholding the claims of an ideal unsuited to his nature the sole cause of his discontent; he exclaims: "What a guilty skunk she made me feel!" And so he killed her. When Hickey at last considers his story in this light, he, who had been willing to take the consequences of an act he thought inspired by love, takes refuge in a plea of insanity—too tender-minded to accept the conclusion that man's feelings are necessarily ambivalent, that he had killed the one he loved because he hated her.

Another figure in the play, Larry Slade, a former anarchist, who is now unsuccessfully seeking peace in philosophical detachment, universalizes and applies to life itself these variations on a single theme, crying out: "There's no hope! I'll never be a success in the grandstand—or anywhere else! Life is too much for me! I'll be a weak fool looking at the two sides of everything till the day I die!"

"The two sides of everything": attraction and repulsion, love and hate, illusion and disillusion, reform and reaction, utopian hope and end-of-an-age despair; these are the well-known materials of modern tragedies, which must end, if the artist fails to see the pattern of justice in "the two sides of everything," as Larry ends, on a note of futility and hopelessness.

The late F. O. Matthiessen praised W. B. Yeats and T. S. Eliot for their mature discovery that we begin to live only when we have conceived life as tragedy. "For both Yeats and Eliot," he wrote, recognize that there can be no significance to life, and hence no tragedy in the account of man's conflicts and his inevitable final defeat by death, unless it is fully realized that there is no such thing as good unless there is also evil, or evil unless there is good; that until this double nature of life is understood by a man, he is doomed to waver between a groundless, optimistic hopefulness and an equally chaotic, pointless despair.

Since many modern writers are either utopian optimists or prophets of disillusion, or both at different times, few have seen that the two sides of everything, good and evil, are the necessary and unalterable poles of human experience, and fewer still have seen or demonstrated the equivalence of hope and fear, joy and sorrow, guilt and remorse, which justifies and makes meaningful our lives. The contrasting moods of illusion and disillusion, of groundless optimism and equally groundless despair, "the two sides of everything," the attraction and repulsion—these the tragedy of ambivalence recognizes but fails to reconcile.

## II

O'Neill is, of course, not the first artist to recognize and use ambivalence. He always proclaimed his great debt to Strindberg, who found women both fascinating and loathsome, and whose ambivalent experiences are reflected in such powerful plays as *The Father*. Hawthorne, who may also have influenced O'Neill, in the conclusion of *The Scarlet Letter* makes an interesting comment on the end of Roger Chillingworth. After the death of Mr. Dimmesdale, the object of his hatred and revenge, Chillingworth's "strength and energy," Hawthorne tells us, all his vital and intellectual force—seemed at once to desert him; insomuch that he positively withered up, shrivelled away, and almost vanished from mortal sight, like an uprooted weed that lies wilting in the sun. . . . It is a curious subject of observation and inquiry, whether hatred and love be not the same thing at bottom. Each, in its utmost development, supposes a high degree of intimacy and heart-knowledge; each renders one individual dependent for the food of his affections and spiritual life upon another. . . . Philosophically considered, therefore, the two passions seem essentially the same.

Indeed, love and hate, joy and sorrow, good and evil are so closely related that it is likely that every man who ever lived has at times viewed persons, things, actions, and even life itself with mixed feelings—attracted and repelled at the same moment. Since these experiences are both common and tragic, it is not surprising that we can find them recorded in Shakespeare's plays. *Hamlet* is an outstanding example. Hamlet's mingled feelings toward his mother are obvious, and one must agree, I think, with A. C. Bradley, first, that Hamlet truly loved Ophelia and, second, that the bitterness bordering on hatred which he shows toward her is not merely a part of his simulation of insanity. The dying Hamlet, by entreating Horatio to live on to tell his story, shows us that his feelings toward life itself are mingled, that although life is not worth living, it is nevertheless worth living well enough to leave a good name behind. "Horatio," he says,

> I am dead;
> Thou livest; report me and my cause aright
> To the unsatisfied.

.   .   .   .   .   .   .   .   .   .   .

## Tragedy

O good Horatio, what a wounded name,
Things standing thus unknown, shall live behind me!
If thou didst ever hold me in thy heart,
Absent thee from felicity awhile,
And in this harsh world draw thy breath in pain,
To tell my story.

### III

One cannot, however, adequately interpret *Hamlet* by
confining his attention to Hamlet's mingled feelings, important though they are. Ambivalence is only an aspect,
a small part, of Shakespearean tragedy. Shakespeare was
a tragic realist who fully understood that "there is no
such thing as good unless there is also evil, or evil unless
there is good." The recognition of ambivalence is part of
this tragic realism. But Shakespeare had a much broader
understanding of human feelings; he saw them as two-
sided always. The great moments in Shakespeare's tragedies bring joy and sorrow together to the hero, in equal
measures determined by his capacity for feeling. When at
the end Lear believes that Cordelia lives, he exclaims:

If it be so,
It is a chance which does redeem all sorrows
That ever I have felt.

Unlike the tragedy of ambivalence, which must end on
a note of futility and confusion because it is a limited view
of the human predicament, Shakespearean tragedy, based
on a fuller understanding of the equivalence of human
feelings, leaves us with the feeling that justice prevails
and thereby reconciles us to life, which at its worst is also
at its best. Shakespeare achieves this marvelous tragic
effect in different ways in different plays, but always the

effect depends upon the equivalence of human feelings. Consider, for example, the tremendous but deeply satisfying ending of *Othello*, in Othello's discovery that Desdemona, whom he has murdered, believing her faithless, was in fact altogether faithful. Here indeed is one of the supreme moments in dramatic literature. No discovery could be more joyful to Othello than the discovery that Desdemona had always been true and loving. And no discovery could be more dreadful than the discovery that it was this faithful and loving Desdemona, and not a strumpet, whom he has killed. Here is the exact equivalence of feelings: the measure of his joy is the measure of his remorse; and no one who views the scene with insight can doubt that the scales of justice, though trembling, are in perfect balance.

## IV

As a final example, let us consider the justice of equivalence as it is revealed in *Macbeth*.

Macbeth is the only hero in the great Shakespearean tragedies whose fall into misery is brought about by deeds which he knows to be evil and evil only, by a course of action which he chooses in the full knowledge that it is against his principles and his better nature. After we have made every possible allowance for the influence of the witches and of Lady Macbeth, the remaining evidence shows clearly that Macbeth's deeds were neither impulsive nor the results of a mere error of judgment; he recognized in advance the principles which he violated and foresaw many of the possible consequences of violating them. Any honest jury would convict him, any honest judge condemn him.

## Tragedy

Although melodramatic rather than tragic, his death at the hands of Macduff and Macduff's appearance with the tyrant's head are appropriate and just; and we can sympathize wholeheartedly with John Masefield's remarks on these incidents in *A Macbeth Production,* published in 1946 and written while the evil deeds of Hitler and Mussolini were fresh in memory. "Modern feeling," wrote Masefield,

is against the bringing on of the head. Actors complain that it makes people laugh; of course it does; the laughter is hysterical, it comes from deep feeling, from relief, that justice has been done. On the stage, in poetry, justice IS done. On your stage show that it IS done; and let all know, certainly, that this time there will not be another war, with war criminals not punished.

If there are wholehearted villains in life, as melodrama assumes, they should come to a bad end, as they invariably do in melodrama. No other ending could satisfy us. Because of his lust for power, Macbeth denied his own principles and chose villainy as his way of life. Aristotle, who thought that the ideal tragic hero is a man, neither eminently virtuous nor totally depraved, whose fall into misery is brought about by a failure to find the mean between extreme courses of action, would have rejected Macbeth as a tragic figure, or at least he would have rejected the Macbeth we have thus far considered.

The Macbeth we have thus far considered is melodramatic rather than tragic. His fate, satisfying as melodrama, lacks the universality and inevitability of tragedy. The true tragic hero is a representative man, whose fate is our fate; we cannot accept Macbeth seen as villain only as a representative man, since we do not regard ourselves as villains and cannot see in the downfall of a scoundrel an adequate symbol of our common destiny. Further-more, the downfall of tyrants, though desirable and satis-fying, is, as we know, not inevitable. Hitler and Mussolini died as Macbeth died, but other tyrants have lived the "lease of nature," and paid their "breath to mortal custom."

There is, however, another Macbeth, or another side to Macbeth—the once loyal and trustworthy Macbeth, whose lust for power makes him susceptible to temptation, but who nevertheless has principles and scruples, the milk of human kindness in his nature, and a desire to do holily what he wishes to do highly. This Macbeth is not a fig-ment of the melodramatic imagination, but a human being and altogether tragic.

At first this Macbeth is so fascinated and horrified by the thought of becoming king through the murder of Duncan that his power to act is smothered. Later he care-fully considers the possible consequences of assassination. He is much less concerned with judgment in the life to come than with the possibility that even-handed justice may prevail here and now. If he murders Duncan, the memories of Duncan's virtues, he reflects, will arouse man-kind against him. If he murders Duncan, he will set an example which will return to plague him; others with some cause will plan to take his life. Finally, if he murders Duncan, the act will be a denial of the principles upon which his honor and renown are based, a monstrous be-trayal of Duncan's threefold trust in him as kinsman, host, and subject. He says,

> I dare do all that may become a man;
> Who dares do more is none.

The all-important question, which Macbeth does not sufficiently consider in his premeditation, is: Can he violate the principles of his better nature without becoming no-man, a nonentity, a spiritual suicide? The play, after the murder of Duncan, is a demonstration of the justice of equivalence: remorse equals guilt; gains made in spite of conscience are canceled by fear of their loss; vice, understood as action in defiance of a man's own better nature, is self-punishment; a good man's principles are his life, and their complete suppression is death.

After Macbeth has chosen between his vaulting ambition and his principles, he is increasingly aware of the significance of his choice. Many images and figures inform us of his realization that he has chosen darkness, blood, night, sleeplessness, and death and sacrificed light, the milk of human kindness, day, sleep, and life. He has gained infamy, slaves, mouth-honor, and curses and lost renown, honor, love, and obedience.

Macbeth's principles and better nature die hard; this fact explains the frenzy which drives him beyond the murder of Banquo and the plan to murder Macduff— both real threats to his power—to the senseless murder of Macduff's wife and son and to other cruel acts mentioned but not described in the play. Had the murder of Duncan transformed him into a hardened villain, with his better nature and principles dead and forgotten, the slaughter of those powerless to harm him would have been quite unnecessary. But because he finds the torture of living with his dying better self unendurable, and because he attributes his agony to the fact that he is as yet young in evil deeds, he hopes to drown his conscience in action. He decides to go the whole hog in villainy, to wade on across a river of blood, to act on evil impulses without reflection.

The rest is the final fulfillment of justice through the living death of the better Macbeth. He says,

> I have lived long enough: my way of life
> Is fall'n into the sear, the yellow leaf.

With the light of his nature fast failing, he takes a last look at life and, describing what he sees, achieves a masterpiece of self-portrayal:

> Life's but a walking shadow, a poor player
> That struts and frets his hour upon the stage
> And then is heard no more: it is a tale
> Told by an idiot, full of sound and fury,
> Signifying nothing.

Such indeed is life without principle. A few flickers of the old Macbeth remain; he decides to die with his harness on his back, and finally, with all odds against him, to die rather than to yield. These last signs of the admirable in him remind us that we are witnessing, not only the downfall of a tyrant, but also the last of a man who, through the inevitable workings of the justice of equivalence, had already paid with his life for the murder of his principles.

## VI ✳

# Romeo and Juliet and A Midsummer Night's Dream: Tragedy and Comedy

AT THE end of Plato's *Symposium* we find an amusing picture of a great philosopher putting Agathon, the tragic poet, and Aristophanes, the greatest comic poet of Athens, to sleep with his discourse on the nature of tragedy and comedy. As Plato tells the story, it happened in the early hours of the morning, after a night spent in feasting and singing the praises of love:

There remained [of the company] only Socrates, Aristophanes, and Agathon, who were drinking out of a large goblet which they passed round, and Socrates was discoursing to them. Aristodemus was only half awake, and he did not hear the beginning of the discourse; the chief thing which he remembered was Socrates compelling the other two to acknowledge that the genius of comedy was the same with that of tragedy, and that the true artist in tragedy was an artist in comedy also. To this they were constrained to assent, being drowsy, and not quite following the argument. And first of all Aristophanes dropped off, then, when the day was already dawning, Agathon. Socrates, having laid them to sleep, rose to depart. [Jowett translation]

Like all good comedy, this scene is entertaining as well as instructive. It is entertaining because it presents the opposite of the order we naturally expect: a tragic poet and a comic poet, whom we expect to be interested in a discourse on the nature of tragedy and comedy, fall asleep; it is instructive because it makes the point, evident elsewhere in literary history, that tragic and comic poets do not need explicitly formulated theories of tragedy and comedy, that they are often indifferent to such abstract speculations.

The distinctive form and significance of tragedies and comedies indicate, however, that the successful poets have had an adequate sense of the tragic and the comic. Apparently the appreciative reader or spectator also possesses this mysterious but adequate sense of the nature of tragedy and comedy, for as the artist can create without an explicitly formulated theory, so the reader can appreciate and enjoy the specific work of art without the benefit of definitions and generalizations. But although speculation about the nature of tragedy and comedy is not indispensable to either creation or appreciation, it is, nevertheless, a natural and, indeed, inevitable result of our curiosity as rational beings. If it did not begin before, dramatic theory began as the first spectators were leaving the first performance in the first theatre. When we have had an intensely interesting experience, we are eager to know its nature and its causes. Why do we enjoy the spectacle of a man who falls from prosperity to adversity? Why do we laugh at fools? As long as we are interested in drama and in its sources in life, we shall be asking these questions and trying to answer them.

The assertion that the genius of tragedy is the same as that of comedy and that the true artist in tragedy is an artist in comedy also is the kind of provocative conundrum or apparent paradox which Socrates loved to discuss. It was a bold speculative assertion rather than a description of known facts, for the Greek dramatic poets, as we know them, kept tragedy and comedy apart and excelled in one or the other, not in both. Plato, who recorded the assertion, supported it in practice by displaying a sharp comic sense in the *Symposium* and a deep tragic sense in the dialogues which describe the trial and death of Socrates. But its support in drama did not come until the 1590's, when Shakespeare wrote *Romeo and Juliet* and *A Midsummer Night's Dream*, displaying genius in both tragedy and comedy.

What did Socrates have in mind? If the genius of tragedy is the same as that of comedy, what is the difference between the two? Certainly, he rejected the popular choice of the distinction between an unhappy and a happy ending as the difference between tragedy and comedy: in Plato's *Philebus* he maintains that we view both forms of drama with mingled pleasure and pain, smiling through our tears at tragedy and responding to the ridiculous in others with laughter, which is pleasant, tinged with envy, which is unpleasant. But this view, although it supports the assertion that tragedy and comedy are similar, leaves us, if both have the same effect, with no way of distinguishing one from the other. It can hardly be all that Socrates had in mind.

After years of wondering what he had in mind when his audience at the symposium failed him, I do not know the answer, but I have reached the point where I know what I should have said if I had been Socrates and if I had been more fortunate than he in holding my audience.

Man, I should have said, is a rational animal: he is always looking for meaning in his experience. He looks for meaning and order everywhere, but since the desire to find some significant pattern in his joys and sorrows, some just relation between good and evil, is closest to his heart, surpassing even his desire to grasp the order of the physical world, he looks most intently for meaning in the realm of values. That is why tragedy, which is an artistic demonstration that justice governs our joys and sorrows, has always seemed to most critics to be the highest form of art.

Since man has only a finite intelligence, he cannot always find the order he craves, either in the inner world of values or in the outer world of science and external description. In his search for order he is everywhere confronted by disorder, absurdity, nonsense, and incongruity. Fortunately, however, he finds in laughter, at least in his relaxed moments, an enjoyable emotional reaction to these disappointments to his reason. We rightly honor the comic poet, who by presenting nonsense in contrast to sense points up the difference between the two and who through laughter reconciles us to those experiences which frustrate the effort of reason to find meaningful patterns in all experience.

*Tragedy*

Order and disorder, the congruous and the incongruous, sense and nonsense, profundity and absurdity are pairs of opposites; each member of each pair throws light on the other so that whoever has a keen sense of order, congruity, sense, and profundity must also have a keen sense of disorder, incongruity, nonsense, and absurdity. Clearly, then, if the discovery of order in the realm of good and evil is the glory of tragedy, which finds intelligibility and justice in our seemingly chance joys and sorrows, and if the glory of comedy lies in its transformation of the frustrations of reason into soothing laughter, the artist in tragedy may also be an artist in comedy, and vice versa; and it may also be said that the genius of tragedy is similar to that of comedy.

Socrates, who was a rationalist, might well have expounded his apparent paradox in this fashion; very probably, however, the rivalry between philosophers and poets in his time would have made it difficult for him to recognize the tragic poets as the discoverers of justice in our joys and sorrows and the comic poets as the teachers of the difference between sense and nonsense. Since we can never know what Socrates had in mind, the final episode of the *Symposium* must remain, as Plato intended, a frustration of reason made pleasant by laughter at the absurdity of the ideal audience falling asleep in the presence of the right speaker on the right subject. This pleasant frustration does not prevent us, however, from determining for ourselves whether the great teacher's provocative conundrum will serve as a key to the meaning of tragedy and comedy.

The hypothesis which I have offered as a substitute for the slumber-stifled discussion needs amplification and verification by specific examples. What better test can be found than the first test afforded by the history of dramatic literature—the appearance of *Romeo and Juliet* and *A Midsummer Night's Dream* as the works of one author? These plays prove that Shakespeare, at least, was an artist in both tragedy and comedy. Do they indicate also that the genius of tragedy is similar to that of comedy? Do they indicate that the two are related as order is related to disorder—that the function of tragedy is to reveal a just order in our joys and sorrows and the function of comedy to turn disorder into soothing laughter?

## II

The answers to two questions lead us directly to the heart of the tragic meaning of *Romeo and Juliet*. The first question is, What causes the downfall of the hero and of the heroine who shares his fate? The second question is, In what sense does the play have universality: does the fate of Romeo and Juliet represent the fate of all lovers?

Shakespeare himself could not have correctly answered the first question—What causes the downfall of the hero and heroine?—before he finished the play. *Romeo and Juliet* is Shakespeare's first true tragedy; as he wrote it, he was developing his own sense of the tragic. He started the play with a view which he found unsatisfactory as he went on writing and ended with a view which he upheld in all his later tragedies. He started with the view that something outside the hero is the cause of his downfall, that something outside man is the cause of the individual's particular fate.

His first view is stressed in the Prologue, which announces that "a pair of star-cross'd lovers take their life."

This forecast points ahead to Romeo's exclamation, when he hears and believes the report of Juliet's death:

Is it even so? then I defy you, stars!

From this point on, every step he takes leads to his downfall. He buys poison from the apothecary, goes to Juliet's tomb, drinks the poison, and dies—while Juliet still lives. The stars are triumphant. Romeo's defiance of his fate hastens its fulfillment.

The stars are symbolic of the elements of bad luck and chance in the action of the play, of the bad luck which involves Romeo in a renewal of the feud and of the chance delay of the messenger who would have told him that Juliet lived. But do the stars, do chance and bad luck, determine the particular fate of the individual? Bad luck and chance are facts of life, but is there a deeper fact than chance and bad luck, a truer cause of the individual's fate? Like Romeo, we all suffer at times from bad luck. Like Romeo, we all hear rumors and alarms and false warnings and reports of danger and disaster. We know from experience that our response to these chance and unlucky events is more important than the events themselves; and our responses depend upon our characters. Character is a deeper and more important influence in human affairs than luck or chance.

Some time ago a radio program presented, as a remarkable illustration of chance and bad luck, the story of a man from Pennsylvania who had been hit by a train three times at the same crossing. When we reflect upon his story, we are likely to conclude that it is a revelation of character rather than an illustration of chance. If we had been in his place, most of us, after the first accident, would have taken all possible precautionary measures to see that it did not happen again; and if by chance we were struck again by an unscheduled train on a day when the crossing signals were not working, it seems likely that we would never again cross the tracks at that point. It is difficult for us to avoid the conclusion that the man from Pennsylvania was the kind of man who gets hit by trains.

Examples of "chance" and "bad luck" are common in the news. The following is representative of many: "A year to the day after he broke his left leg in a fall caused by a loose plank in his doorstep, John Jones, 47, of . . . , broke his right leg when he tripped over the same plank." Obviously, this is another revelation of character: Jones is the kind of man who will risk another leg rather than fix the plank.

While writing his first tragedy, Shakespeare discovered that the individual's fate is determined from within, by character, and not from without, by chance or bad luck. Although the character of Romeo is not as clearly revealed as the characters of Lear, Hamlet, Macbeth, and Othello, it is nevertheless certain from a point early in the play that Romeo is the kind of person who is inclined to accept bad news at its face value and who is inclined, when he is confronted by apparent disaster, toward some despairing deed. In his despair when the feud broke out —at a time when he knew that Juliet lived—he would have killed himself if the Nurse and Friar Laurence had not prevented him from so doing. Since the Nurse and Friar Laurence could not always be present in his despairing moments and since the temptations to despair are all too common in life, it was with Romeo only a matter of time.

## Tragedy

The stars remain in *Romeo and Juliet,* as well as the chance and bad luck of which they are symbols, but the play also offers a better explanation for the downfall of Romeo. It suggests that "a man's character is his fate," as Heraclitus said—a dictum which sums up one pattern of tragic meaning, one aspect of the tragic poet's vision of order in the universe.

In all his later plays, Shakespeare looked within to character, and not to the stars or to chance or luck, for the causes of individual fates:

> The fault, dear Brutus, is not in our stars,
> But in ourselves, that we are underlings.

We come now to the second question: How is the fate of Romeo and Juliet representative of the fate of all lovers: in what sense does the play have universality?

In looking for the answer to this question, we should first notice how neatly balanced are the feelings of the principals in the play. Taking love as a representative emotional experience, Shakespeare stresses both sides of the experience—the joy and exaltation of the lovers when they are united and their anxiety and unhappiness when they are separated. We see the lovers at both extremes of feeling. The balanced pyramidal form of the play, the five-act structure with the turn at the middle following the rise and fall of the fortunes of the principals, parallels the balance between joy and sorrow which Shakespeare's insight finds in human experience. The artistic structure of the play is an outward show of its inner meaning.

In *Romeo and Juliet* the ending is a dramatic summing up of the whole action: the death of the lovers is symbolical of their lives. Each realizes at the end the extremes of good and evil. In one sense they are united forever, as they wished to be; in another sense they are separated forever in death. Here we see not a happy ending, as in a fairy story, and not an unhappy ending, as in some grim naturalistic tale, in which the worm finally is stilled after wriggling on the hook, but a truly tragic ending, in which joy and sorrow are inevitably joined together—a victory in defeat, a victory of the human spirit accompanied by the inevitable defeat of finite human beings.

Shakespearean tragedy is an artistic vision and revelation of a kind of divine justice which regulates the lives of men and women. Through poetic insight, Shakespeare finds a pattern, an order, in the realm of values; through insight he measures the extremes of feeling, which cannot be measured in any other way. Whoever sees in Shakespearean tragedy only a spectacle of suffering, only an unhappy ending, is seeing only half the story, only one side of life. The artist has done his best to present the whole story and both sides of life. For in the relation between the poles of experience, good and evil, he finds order in the universe. First, he finds that the individual fate of the hero is determined by character, not by chance. Second, he finds that the universality of the hero rests on the fact that, like all of us, the hero is fated to experience the extremes of feeling; and, in accordance with his capacity for feeling, in something like balanced and equal measures, when we follow the rise and fall of the hero's fortunes, we feel ourselves joined to him and to all mankind in the justice of a common fate: this is the secret of the reconciliation to suffering which we find in tragedy.

## III

At the time of writing *Romeo and Juliet* and *A Midsummer Night's Dream,* Shakespeare must have been deeply impressed by the thought that the same material —the theme of love, for example, or life itself—may be treated as either tragic or comic. At the beginning of *A Midsummer Night's Dream,* the Athenian lovers, Hermia and Lysander, are in a predicament as serious as the plight of Romeo and Juliet; well may Lysander say, "The course of true love never did run smooth." But the roughness in the course of their love turns out to be the laughable ups and down of comedy while the roughness in the course of Romeo's love turns into a profoundly tragic change of fortune. The story of Pyramus and Thisbe, the play within a play in *A Midsummer Night's Dream* is, in its main outlines, the same as the story of Romeo and Juliet, yet it becomes in production, as Hippolyta says, "the silliest stuff that ever I heard," while the story of Romeo and Juliet becomes in production a great demonstration that order and justice prevail.

What difference in treatment of the same material— what difference in point of view toward the same material—makes possible the difference between comedy and tragedy?

*A Midsummer Night's Dream* presents the theme of love on three levels: the level of common sense; the level of nonsense, incongruity, and absurdity; and the level of fantasy. The level of common sense is represented by the love and marriage of Theseus and Hippolyta, who provide the necessary contrast to nonsense. The level of nonsense is represented by the Athenian lovers, Lysander,

Demetrius, Helena, and Hermia, and by the workmen, Quince, Snug, Bottom, Flute, Snout, and Starveling, who turn the tragic story of Pyramus and Thisbe into a comic revelation of their own inadequacies. The level of fantasy is represented by the loves of Titania and Oberon, and by the juice of the flower called love-in-idleness, which here serves Shakespeare as an explanation of the influence of chance, caprice, and propinquity on love between the sexes. Since two of these levels, sense and nonsense, are always represented in all comedies, they deserve a few words of comment and definition.

The world of sense is the world of orderly and meaningful patterns, both rational and conventional. Its first law is the law of identity, namely, A is A, which "simply expresses the fact that every term and idea which we use in our reasonings" and practical calculations "must remain what it is." Shakespeare, for example, can make "sense" of the world of human values and find a just order in it only if the law of identity holds true. A is A; and if Romeo is Romeo—that is, if we can be sure that Romeo's character does not change or will not change, then we can understand his fate or even in a general way predict it. Similarly, if for Romeo good is to-be-united-with-Juliet and evil is to-be-separated-from-her—if his values do not change—then we can see in the rise and fall of his fortunes a just balance between good and evil.

The world of nonsense is, in contrast, governed by a law which is the exact opposite of the law of identity. A is not always A; A is sometimes B, or C, or D; and for this reason the world of nonsense is a world of disorder and incongruities. The laughable absurdities and incongruities in *A Midsummer Night's Dream* are for the most part direct consequences of this law of change of identity. Every change of identity leads to incongruities or comic ups and downs. Lysander, for example, is first presented to us as the lover of Hermia; later, touched by the juice of the magic flower, he becomes the lover of Helena; still later through magic he becomes the lover of Hermia again: A becomes B, and then becomes A again. Helena, we are told, was once the object of Demetrius' love; she is first presented to us as an unloved maiden; later through magic she is the object of Lysander's love, later still the object of the love of both Lysander and Demetrius; and finally the object of Demetrius' love only. A becomes B, and then becomes C, and then becomes D, and finally becomes A again. And so on with the Athenian lovers.

In contrast, Theseus and Hippolyta, who represent sense, remain what they are throughout the play.

Bottom, that king of the world of nonsense, undergoes a series of "translations." An ass in the eyes of the audience from the beginning, but a man of parts to his fellows, he later becomes through magic an ass in appearance, later the object of Titania's doting, later still the object of her loathing, and later still Bottom once more. Meanwhile, to complicate the scheme, he wishes to become Pyramus in the play, and also Thisbe, and also Lion. (I'll spare you the working out of his "translations" in ABC's.)

The most effective comedy in *A Midsummer Night's Dream* comes from the subtle use of change of identity in the production of the play within the play, "Pyramus and Thisbe." In the world of sense we accept the convention whereby the actor assumes the identity of the part he plays. In the theatre Brian Aherne is Romeo, Katharine Cornell is Juliet. Not so in "Pyramus and Thisbe": Shakespeare reverses the convention and changes order into disorder and incongruity, so that the production excites in us uproarious laughter rather than tragic sympathy and insight. Following the convention of the theatre, we would accept Lion and forget the actor, but Lion insists on telling us that he is not Lion but Snug the joiner. Similarly, by every device at his command, Shakespeare makes certain that we cannot see Pyramus, Thisbe, Wall, Moonshine, and Lion because we must see Snug, Bottom, Flute, Snout, and Starveling. By such devices, based on change of identity, first principle in the world of nonsense and incongruity, what might be seen as tragedy must be seen as comedy.

If tragedy reveals significant patterns in experience, demonstrating that character is fate and that men are united in the justice which apportions equal measures of joy and sorrow to each individual, and if comedy reconciles us through laughter to the disorder, the nonsense, the incongruities and absurdities which we meet everywhere in experience, how does the artist, working with the same material, with love or with life itself, make the choice between comedy and tragedy and determine whether we shall respond to his work of art with laughter or with tragic insight? Shakespeare must have thought of this question in some form while he was writing *Romeo and Juliet* and *A Midsummer Night's Dream;* and possibly his answer is to be found in the reply of Theseus to Hippolyta's verdict on the workers' production of "Pyramus and Thisbe": Hippolyta exclaimed, "This is the silliest stuff that ever I heard." And Theseus replied, "The best in this kind are but shadows, and the worst are no worse, if imagination amend them." If there exists anywhere a wiser comment on drama and the theatre, I have not read or heard it.

Undoubtedly Shakespeare must have been thinking, as he wrote the reply of Theseus to Hippolyta, that the same imagination which willingly accepts actors as Romeo, or Hamlet, or Macbeth, or Lear, that accepts the past as the present, the stage as a series of faraway places, and fiction as life itself, could also accept, if it were permitted to do so, his "Pyramus and Thisbe." He knew that his "Pyramus and Thisbe," with the incongruities in the diction removed, and with competent actors losing themselves in their parts (including Lion, Moonshine, and Wall), could be successfully presented as tragedy. For he knew that the chief difference between "silly stuff" and profound art is caused by the artist's power to enlist the spectator's imagination. We can be sure that he knew this because in "Pyramus and Thisbe," as we see it, he has deliberately frustrated, for the sake of laughter, our imagination and prevented us at every point from amending the inherent limitations of drama.

Perhaps he was thinking also of the wider question of what difference in the artist's point of view determines whether we shall focus our attention on the underlying order in experience or on its superficial disorder and incongruities. Can the answer be found in imagination understood as sympathetic insight?

In "Pyramus and Thisbe" we are never permitted to see the story from the point of view of the lovers themselves; we see it only from the outside, as detached and unsympathetic observers. Indeed, we are not permitted to see the lovers at all: we see only the incongruity of the workers presuming to play the parts of a highborn couple. Again, we see the Athenian lovers only from the outside. Hermia, Lysander, Demetrius, and Helena—each is identified for us only as the object of another's affection. They have no inwards for us, and since this is so, how can we possibly tell, from watching them, whether character is fate or whether each suffers and enjoys in equal measures?

Our experience in witnessing *Romeo and Juliet* is altogether different. Soon after the beginning, we follow the action with sympathetic insight from within, from the point of view of the lovers themselves. Inwardness— where character and values may be found and measured by insight—becomes for us the only reality. We live with Romeo and Juliet, seeing the world with their eyes, and as we rise and fall with their fortunes, we are carried finally beyond envy and pity and filled with a sense that all men share a common fate.

## IV

Can we say, then, that life is comic if we view it chiefly from the outside, as detached observers whose attention is focused mainly on the disorder and incongruities of the surface? And can we say that life is tragic when we view it from within, from the point of view of an individual— our own point of view or that of someone with whom we identify ourselves by sympathetic insight, as we do with Romeo and Juliet?

Walpole's famous dictum that "the world is a comedy to those that think, a tragedy to those who feel" on first consideration may seem to sum up satisfactorily at this point, for the detached, outer view of man, which permits us to smile at nonsense and incongruity, is at least partially the kind of objectivity which we associate with thought. And sympathetic insight, indispensable in the appreciation of tragedy, obviously involves us in the world of feelings and values. But Walpole's equation of the difference between comedy and tragedy with the difference between thought and feeling does not take into account that, in the first place, laughter is itself an emotion and that, therefore, our response even to "pure" comedy is emotional. Secondly, the emotion of laughter mixes freely with other emotions, and this fact explains the existence of various kinds of comedy.

When the comic poet is amused by someone or something that he dislikes, the result is satire; when he is amused by someone or something that he likes, the result is humor. The spirit of *A Midsummer Night's Dream,* for example, is one of good humor rather than of satire. Shakespeare, we feel, likes human beings even while he laughs at them and is not motivated by a desire to change their ways. Their ways, especially the ways of lovers, are often absurd and nonsensical, but Shakespeare does not view these absurdities as a stern moralist or a cynic might.

*A Midsummer Night's Dream* is saved from cynicism by the third level of the comedy—the level of fantasy, the imaginative level which softens the sharp distinctions between the world of sense and the world of nonsense. If all the changes of identity on the part of the lovers were attributed to caprice and propinquity, the result would be cynicism, but most of them are attributed to magic in the world of fantasy, and the result is a softer, kindlier humor, which transforms our rational distress at chance and disorder into soothing laughter. There is insight in the background of *A Midsummer Night's Dream,* as in all great comedy. The magic juice of the flower called love-in-idleness seems to tell us that if only we knew the true causes of what seems to be mere chance and caprice in affairs of the heart, then even these apparent absurdities would make sense to us. The fact that it is a creature from fairyland, not a man, who exclaims: "Lord, what fools these mortals be!" takes the poison out of the comment.

Nor can tragedy be satisfactorily explained as the view of a man who is only a man of feeling—if such a man exists. Tragedy can best be explained by its appeal to our rational craving for order, for patterns of meaning; it satisfies this craving at the important point where our reason and our feelings unite. Tragedy offers a vision of order in the universe, which we grasp with sympathetic insight and respond to emotionally as we rise and fall, or fall and rise, with the hero's fortunes. Furthermore, tragedy requires artistic objectivity as well as insight. Sympathetic insight alone might tempt Shakespeare—who as artist enjoys the omnipotence of a creator—to save Romeo from the fate which inevitably flows from his character, but artistic objectivity will not permit him to do so. Even Zeus must bow to necessity.

The spectator also views serious drama with a combination of insight and artistic objectivity, and he applauds the tragic artist who offers both as greater than the writer who is tempted by sympathy to sacrifice objectivity and provide us with a happy ending. We readily recognize such writings as one-sided, as untrue to life, as appeals to our weakness.

Thought and feeling are involved in the creation and

appreciation of both comedy and tragedy. In seeing each, we experience an intellectual awareness accompanied by appropriate emotional responses. The main difference is that in tragedy our intelligence is directed toward order in the universe; in comedy, toward disorder and incongruity. Without sympathetic insight, we cannot behold the tragic vision of the fate common to all men. Without detachment, we cannot realize the effect of comedy, which transforms the frustrations of reason into laughter. But there is objectivity as well as insight in the tragic vision, and there is always insight in the background of great comedy. The difference between the point of view of tragedy and that of comedy cannot, therefore, be equated simply with the difference between insight and detachment, but rather is to be found in a subtler proportion whereby insight is stressed in tragedy and detachment is stressed in comedy.

# PART THREE

# Toward a Tragic View of Life

# VII ⁕

# Heroes and the Way
# of Compromise

IN A BRIEF and pointed imaginary conversation between Frederick the Great and the utopian pacifists of his own time, William James once epitomized the almost comic clash between the attitude of the hero and that of the extreme advocates of moderation. " 'Dogs, would you live forever?' shouted Frederick the Great. 'Yes,' say our utopians, 'let us live forever, and raise our level gradually.' "

History in the making today offers to the student of human affairs another chapter, already half-written, in the ancient conflict between extremism and moderation. We are perhaps too close to our world to determine the prime cause, if indeed there be one only, of its division into warring camps. One clue, however, is to be found in the events leading up to World War II: the worship of half-truths which made some peoples seek the heroic life as a national ideal while others sought to live by compromise alone.

Frederick, in spite of his fierce scorn, must have been clever enough to see how much he owed to the moderate men of his own time, who served him as foils. Looking back on the events of the past thirty years, we can see that our own Fredericks owed much of their success in enthralling the spirit of great nations to the fortune which made them loom large against a pale background of peoples who seemed to have lost the courage to face the fact that a willingness to die is sometimes the price of a life worth the living. The hero is always dramatic; the moderate is colorless by contrast, and especially so when he loudly proclaims his revulsion from every form of the heroic spirit.

What happens to a world in which the lines are sharply drawn between extremists and moderate men? Part of the answer is already written. First, the extremist forces his way of life upon his fellows. In the pursuit of his goal, whatever it may be, life is a bright coin which he is willing, at any moment, to exchange for glorious death; he scorns those who believe that a long and peaceful life is the only reasonable goal. In dealing with him, moderate men discover that compromise is not true compromise, but appeasement. Those who make this discovery have a choice between two equally extreme courses of action. Either they may themselves take heroic measures against the fanatic who will not compromise or they may persist in the error of appeasement until it becomes nihilism, the denial of the heroic in life which men sometimes pay for by losing their freedom and even their lives.

Living witnesses to this process, all the great nations were committed during World War II to the heroic way of life. Each was determined to fight on to victory or to death. Some sincerely believed that the moderate way of compromise is the only true way for men and for nations; but first, before they could think of ideal procedures, there was a job to be done, someone to be blotted out, someone with whom compromise was impossible.

After World War II, what? Freed from the menace of some of the new Fredericks, the moderates will presumably go back to the business of raising their level gradually. For some time they will have a new respect for *some* heroes, for those who successfully led them against the would-be world conquerors; but this new respect may easily vanish in the inevitable reaction against "blood, sweat, and tears." Will our utopians increase the power and menace of the remaining Caesars by again insisting that the way of compromise is always the best way of life?

We cannot correct the past mistakes which brought Caesarism into our world. The generation which turned moderation itself into a new form of extremism by refusing to find a place in their scheme of things for the heroic human spirit has done its work. But it is never too late to bring the lessons of experience to bear upon the future. A better understanding of human nature may yet save us from repeating old mistakes

## II

Dramatic poetry is a wonderful storehouse of the lessons of experience and possibly the best source of information concerning heroes and the heroic spirit. By an apparent paradox of intellectual history, the doctrine of the Superman, which exalts intensity of experience, and the philosophy of moderation, which aims chiefly at a long and complete life, were both derived from a study of the tragic hero. In the *Poetics* Aristotle described the extremism of the tragic hero as an error, a failure to find the moderate way, which causes his downfall. In *The Birth of Tragedy* Nietzsche concluded that only as an aesthetic phenomenon is life eternally justified, a conclusion which he expanded in his later writings into the view that life is worth the living only for the Superman, only for the tragic hero who lives dangerously, who risks all to gain all, who touches the heights and depths of experience.

*The Birth of Tragedy* was Nietzsche's first book. In tragedy he discovered the apparent explanation of his youthful admiration for Richard Wagner's heroic music; from a study of tragedy he derived the conclusions that have strongly influenced so many movements in modern society, movements ranging in intensity from the violence and brutality of the Nazi party to the relatively mild "strenuous life" advocated by Theodore Roosevelt.

According to his own account, Nietzsche at first undertook his study of tragedy to answer a question which seemed more likely to interest the scholars and philologists among whom he moved than to unsettle the world of affairs. Did their interest in tragedy indicate that the

Greeks were a pessimistic or decadent people? Nietzsche decided, on the contrary, that tragedy represents the highest degree of affirmation and acceptance of life. In the years which saw the production of the great Attic tragedies the Greeks were a strong people, capable of facing reality at its worst without flinching.

In seeking the answer to his question Nietzsche contracted a raging fever of hero worship. The question of Greek pessimism widened out in his mind into the more important question of whether life is worth living. Most spectators of a great tragedy leave with a sense of reconciliation, with the feeling that life, though terrible, is just. On this point Nietzsche made an important reservation. Life is worth living, he decided, only for the extremist, only for the hero who reaches the heights and depths of feelings. Upon completing his study of tragedy, the future prophet of the Superman was prepared with the outlines of his message. Do you wish to make life worth living? Then love your fate; live dangerously and on the heights; be an extremist, a hero, a superman.

Nietzsche was fascinated by the intensity of the hero's experience, but Aristotle was more deeply impressed by its brevity. The simple fact revealed by tragedy is that heroes always live dangerously and usually do not live long. A comparison of Aristotle's remarks on the tragic hero in the *Poetics* with his theory of the golden mean in the *Nichomachean Ethics* shows the important influence of his study of dramatic poetry on his doctrine of moderation. Since heroes usually do not live long, the extremism which brings about their end is an error of judgment, a tragic failure in conduct. It is an error and a failure because happiness is not to be found in intensity of feeling but only in full self-realization, which requires a long and complete life. "For one swallow does not make a summer, nor does one day; and so too one day, or a short time, does not make a man blessed and happy." Virtue is the very opposite of the error of the tragic hero; it lies in the habit of choosing a mean between extremes, in the moderation which usually secures length of life.

Individual temperament is probably the only explanation for the paradoxical manner in which Aristotle and Nietzsche drew opposite conclusions from the same evidence. Quite clearly, one placed the highest value on the duration and completeness of experience, and the other placed it on intensity. The tragic hero, whose experience is intense, narrow, and brief, is a failure in the eyes of Aristotle and the ideal man in the eyes of Nietzsche.

The opposition between the cult of hero worship, which leads to Caesarism, and the philosophy of moderation, when it is carried to the extreme of nihilism, turns on the question of which quality of experience—intensity or duration—is more desirable. Aristotle himself never carried his doctrine of moderation to the extreme of nihilism. At the risk of inconsistency, he admitted that the virtuous man will sometimes prefer a swallow to a summer: "It is true of the good man too that he does many acts for the sake of his friends and his country, and if necessary dies for them . . . since he would prefer a short period of intense pleasure to a long one of mild enjoyment, a twelve-month of noble life to many years of humdrum existence, and one great and noble action to many trivial ones." The whole truth about human nature, as an answer to this question, can be derived from the same evidence from which the contradictory half-truths of hero worship and nihilism have been derived.

## III

The tragic hero has enough in common with other men to make his fate significant to them, and at the same time is unusual enough to excite and hold their interest. His difference, which is the secret of his dramatic interest, is his intensity, which is first manifest in his unyielding purpose. The first quality which distinguishes the hero is the will to do or die, the uncompromising spirit which makes him pay any price, even life itself, for his object. It is this quality which Wolfe at Quebec has in common with Marlowe's Tamburlaine, which Stonewall Jackson shares with Melville's Captain Ahab. In itself it is without moral significance, for the unyielding hero may be either a saint or a sinner in the eyes of the spectator. But unyielding character is the spring from which heroic and dramatic actions flow.

The hero's attitude toward life is that of Ahab toward the whale; not even the gods can swerve him from his purpose. "Over unsounded gorges, through the rifled hearts of mountains, under torrents' beds, unerringly I rush! Naught's an obstacle, naught's an angle to the iron way!" Such intensity demands concentration, and Ahab's purpose is centered on a single object, Moby Dick. "Ay, ay!" he cries, "and I'll chase him round Good Hope, and round the Horn, and round the Norway Maelstrom, and round perdition's flames before I give him up." And so it always is with heroes: each has his favorite phantom, always something specific, never an abstraction. The hero does not die for love, or for power, or for success, or for revenge:

137

he dies for Juliet, or for Abbie, or for Rautendelein, or for Desdemona; he dies to be Duncan's successor or for "infinite riches in a little room"; he dies to climb the tower that he has built. The hero is indeed always a monomaniac to some extent, but he is different from his fellow men only in degree, not in kind, only in the intensity with which he pursues his object.

In life and in drama the heroic is marked by an uncompromising will; in both, moreover, the difference between the simplest and the greatest is that the greatest brings the widest range of feeling and the highest intellectual power to bear upon his inflexible purpose. Such is the difference between Grant in the Wilderness and Lincoln in the White House, between Tamburlaine and Hamlet. Grant's determination to fight it out on one line is as firm as Lincoln's will to carry through the war, but Lincoln adds to fundamental determination an intellectual power made manifest in his brooding on the meaning of events, as in the Gettysburg and Second Inaugural addresses, and a wide range of feeling which carries him into the hearts of all the actors in the national tragedy. His acts of kindness to delinquent soldiers, his concern for the point of view of his opponents, his letter to Mrs. Bixby— make more pointed, more heroic, more valuable his determination to save the Union. We rightly value the heroic according to its cost to the hero; and a Hamlet, to whom the cost is so great as to make him seem at times weak in will, displays a richer heroism in one moment of tortured struggle than can be found in all the thoughtless, insensate fury of a Tamburlaine.

## IV

Such is the nature of the hero; what are its inevitable consequences? If we may trust the testimony of all serious drama, the outstanding consequence is that the hero lives intensely but not long. Life is the price we must all pay for experience; most of us dole it out in little sums over a long period of time; the hero gladly pays in a lump sum.

A more profoundly significant consequence is that the hero always gets what he wants—and always pays the full price. Oedipus finds the unknown murderer, at a cost; Wolfe takes Quebec, but falls in the moment of victory; Ahab throws the harpoon, and dies; Romeo comes back to Juliet, in death. The hero can have anything he wants, for a price; but not even a hero can get something for nothing.

Drama reveals these consequences in many ways—by showing that the hero falls as far as he rises or that he is brought down by the very forces which bring him to the top. The great turn of the wheel of fortune which carries the hero to the extremes of joy and grief, often in one moment of dazzling intensity, is the dramatic symbol of the endless little ups and downs, the little sorrows and joys, of ordinary men. The hero's great moment contains within itself rise and fall, fortune and misfortune, triumph and disaster. As Ahab at last faces the white whale alone, he cries: "Oh, now I feel my topmost greatness lies in my topmost grief." Othello's fate is wonderfully balanced in the moment of his discovery of Desdemona's innocence. For him this discovery means sheer exaltation; and yet this exaltation must come to him balanced by the horror of his own crime. Joy and sorrow are balanced with a ter-

*139*

rible nicety, that wonderful balance which Edgar in *King Lear* notes in speaking of the death of his father:

> his flaw'd heart,—
> Alack, too weak the conflict to support!—
> 'Twixt two extremes of passion, joy and grief,
> Burst smilingly.

All these qualities suit the hero to the purposes and necessities of dramatic poetry. Some attempts have been made to dispense with the hero in serious drama. Maeterlinck says in a famous essay on tragedy:

I have grown to believe that an old man, seated in his armchair, waiting patiently, with his lamp beside him . . . I have grown to believe that he, motionless as he is, does yet live in reality a deeper, more human, and more universal life than the lover who strangles his mistress, the captain who conquers in battle, or "the husband who avenges his honor."

That the old man is as tragic as the hero, no one should question: he too has his moments; he too pays for what he gets. If it were not so, if he were not tragic in this sense, then the hero of tragic drama could have no universal significance. The trouble with the old man in the armchair is that he is tragic but not dramatic. His life has meaning but lacks every other dramatic quality; intensity, suspense, surprise, reversal, heightened diction, power to excite basic feelings—all are missing. When we think of the tragic in terms of the two-sided nature of feeling which is the basis of the common destiny of men, one man is as good an illustration as another, but only the intense hero makes drama possible, and makes it possible for it to end within two hours.

After we have looked at enough heroes, we can readily

understand Aristotle's reaction to their way of life. He sees the hero for what he is, if the ultimate standard of conduct is length and completeness of life: a man not "eminently good and just, yet whose misfortune is brought about not by vice or depravity, but by some error or frailty." No doubt this tragic flaw is simply the essential nature of the hero—his extremism. No hero ever chose the golden mean in a critical moment; no hero would ever sacrifice his purpose or any part of the "iron way" to the dictates of the kind of reason and virtue which bring length of life.

## V

Great drama itself is not an adverse criticism of the way of heroes. Only confirmed Aristotelians believe that it is. Through his hero the dramatist is enabled to present the essence of life; and from the character of the hero and his fate we may draw our own conclusions. One famous exception is Ibsen's *Brand*, which was deliberately intended to be an attack on the heroic way of life. Brand, the fanatic priest, demands of all those about him, of his family and of his parishioners, the same heroic devotion to God and negation of the world which he himself seeks to practice. These demands result ultimately in the ruin of his family, the revolt of his flock, and his own death. But Ibsen is able to make the case neither better nor worse for the hero than have all great tragedies. Particularly interesting about the play, however, is what Ibsen, as a great dramatist, thought about the nature of the hero. This is revealed in two phrases, one positive, the other negative. "All or nothing," says Brand again and again to his followers in demanding their devotion. And warning them ever and again of evil, he repeats: "The devil is compromise."

From *Brand* we might conclude that Ibsen ascribed the woes of mankind to the iron way of heroes. But in *Peer Gynt,* his poetic satire on the Norwegian character, he wrote an even more impressive criticism of the way of compromise. The play was written out of the depths of Ibsen's indignation with Norway for her failure to ally herself with Denmark in the Danish-Prussian war. Peer Gynt is the opposite of Brand. "Enough," is his motto, not "all or nothing." His method is to go around obstacles and to abandon projects, ideals, and objectives when they seem to demand the ultimate risk. Since, in following this method, he wanders over the face of the earth, he seems to have led a richer life than Brand, who fights it out with the devil of compromise within the narrow confines of his parish. In the end, however, Peer is revealed as one who stands for nothing, a man without principles or character, a nonentity. Like the objects of Thoreau's pity, he has frittered away his life in detail. One could say to him, as to the little mouse who was granted his wish to have wings: "You're nothing but a nothing; you're not a thing at all."

All drama reminds us that it is a serious mistake to underestimate the power of the heroic or to assume that people see only the unpleasant consequences of the way of heroes and none of its compensations. The reverse is more often true. "Hero worship" is a familiar term, but there is no similar familiar term to denote reverence for the moderate man. Great drama excites not only pity and terror, but also awe and admiration, and other feelings that lie so deep that we cannot easily name them. Most of the power of the dramatic to excite deep feeling rests in the hero. In him we see ourselves on a larger scale, often ourselves as we should like to be, for who would not like to be firmer of purpose, more intent intellectually, capable of deeper feeling? While we hunger for more of life, we cannot resist the appeal of the hero's intensity. We necessarily have our moments when Aristotle's golden mean seems to be indeed a kind of "golden meanness," a doctrine for the half-hearted who shrink from the farther reaches of experience, a prescription for a long life and a dull one, a guiding principle for a world of old men dozing in armchairs.

## VI

Powerful indeed is hero worship. If drama were possible only in the form of tragic poetry, one might agree with Plato in ruling poets out of the ideal state. Tragedy by itself is an incomplete picture of life; since it presents only heroes to us, it needs comedy as an antidote to the unbridled hero worship which at times it might otherwise cause. Comedy, which teaches us to know a fool when we see one, teaches us also that not any fool can be a hero. The ordinary man, taking his stand on a trivial issue in his efforts to ape the hero, succeeds in being merely sullen. Or if he is, like Nietzsche, a gentle and serious young scholar, an intuitive but humorless philologist, too long fed on a diet of tragic poetry and Wagnerian music, he goes forth as a prophet to trouble the world with dreams of life aesthetically justified by a race of tragic heroes and to bring himself to madness.

To go with Oedipus, we need the Dionysos of *The Frogs;* to go with Hamlet, we need Falstaff; to go with the Cid, we need Orgon. A main effect of *The Frogs* is to show what happens to Dionysos, a sturdy but moderate middle-class soul who sets out to play the part of Hercules, a hero. If the point sinks in, we think twice before aping the way of heroes. As for Falstaff—he is neither a hero nor a fool: he knows how his kind of person should behave on a battlefield; and so, without shame, he lies down to play dead until the heroes have done their work. Orgon *is* a fool, who would never escape the machinations of Tartuffe were it not for the intervention of the king's officer. His folly, which takes the form of worship of the extreme forms of piety, makes him an ideal dupe for a hypocrite.

We may thank the comic spirit for deflating the pseudoheroic in life, and enlist it always in our service against the triumph of the simplest kind of hero, who has intensity of purpose without a correspondingly great capacity for thought and feeling. Such heroes, who are always without humor themselves, flourish in the absence of laughter. Meredith long ago pointed out that the comic spirit is an enemy of the sentimental, of the puritanical, and of the bacchanalian: it is even more strongly the sworn foe of the pseudoheroic and of the kind of hero whose brutality is the result of a will unguided by thought and feeling.

## VII

Between great science, which seeks to show us *nature as it is,* caring nothing for what *it should be,* and great poetry, which has always shown us *human nature as it is,* caring nothing for what the reader thinks *it should be,* there can be no quarrel. But science in its beginnings had to contend with the pretensions of poets in the realm of nature; and today men neglect the solid realities of poetry for the vaporings of rhapsodists, who rest their dreams of progress toward Utopia upon their faith in the ability of science to do the impossible. It pleases us to smile at the pretensions of the philosopher-poet, Heraclitus, who thought that a new sun is born each day in the heavens. We see the folly of trying to make poetry do the work of mathematics. But the rhapsodists of our world are not poets who seek to take over the province of science; rather they are the pseudo scientists who, either in ignorance of or in defiance of the storehouse of wisdom to be found in poetry, would persuade us that the changes which man has been able to effect in his environment foreshadow even more wonderful changes in human nature itself. We have much to learn from both science and poetry. Science has taught us that the same old sun rises daily; the ancient wisdom of poetry is that it shines, and will always shine, upon the same old race of men—upon moderate men, heroes, and fools alike.

On one point Nietzsche was truly inspired: he saw that there is no place in a culture for tragic poetry once men have convinced themselves that they can change the basic conditions of their lives. For tragic poetry steels us to face evil as an inevitable aspect of experience; and it has no place in our culture if we believe that science and technology can free us from evil. Tragic poetry teaches us that each man pursues his own specific good, and that all too often the desire of two or more men for the same object makes conflict a brute fact in human affairs. Of what use is tragic poetry if we are bemused by the Socratic dream of a universal good acceptable to all and sharable by all? Tragic poetry teaches us that fanatics who seek an absolute good for mankind bring down upon men, by an inevitable recoil, their deepest sufferings. Of what use is tragic poetry, if madmen, lusting for personal power, convince us that paradise on earth will be possible once we have submitted ourselves to their wills?

This is the ancient wisdom of poetry which history today confirms: human nature is unchanging, and heroes, fools, and moderate men are always with us. Each of us, indeed, may be fated to play all of these roles in turn, and sometimes more than one role at once. There is often a comic view of even the admirable hero: the Socrates of *The Clouds,* snub-nosed, bald, homely as a gargoyle, absent-minded and absurd in his reasoning, is based upon life, as is the Socrates of the Dialogues. The world has decided that Plato has given us the truer measure of the man, but we should not forget the other portrait. Such twin portraits are often possible. When Rostand sought to follow Hugo's injunction to create heroes who would exhibit the contrast of the sublime and grotesque to be found in life itself, he wrote *Cyrano de Bergerac,* calling it a "heroic comedy" in order to point out that the heroic and the comic can in unusual instances go hand in hand. Cyrano, who says that he seeks "to be always admirable in all things," is a hero to outdo the ordinary hero, who is extreme in one thing only. "Everything to excess," a principle that is fantastic yet heroic, guides Cyrano's every act. When he fights, he fights a hundred men; when he is generous, he gives away all his money; when he is witty, he composes a ballade while fighting a duel. Spectators are so carried away by a blend of laughter and admiration that at the end no one can say which symbol is truer to the man, the grotesque, huge nose which makes him

comic in appearance or the heroic plume which he wears
in his hat, carrying it in death still unsmirched.

## VIII

Are all men likely ever to agree that either intensity
or duration is the higher value in experience? Not until
the past is a completely false guide to the future; not until
tragic poetry is completely out of touch with human nature. Since we have no grounds on which to predict the
coming of a new kind of man, except the say-so of those
romantic utopians who mistake science for magic, we
must continue to think in terms of men as they are. In a
world in which the fanatical extremist is a hardy perennial,
always to be reckoned with, we must fortify ourselves with
wisdom for the moment when our turn may come to play,
as best we can, the part of heroes.

Since most men prefer a long life even at the expense
of stretches of dullness, the Aristotelian golden mean
points to the sensible course for men and nations most
of the time. But if only one issue in a lifetime compels
the moderate man to take a heroic stand, that is the one
moment that fixes his place in history as either a man
or a nonentity.

The trick is to know the right time and the right issue.
No rule is possible. The simple hero is driven on by inflexible character. The fool mistakes the time and is merely
sullen over trifles.

The moment when moderate men take a stand is always
grave, but it is not a time for despair. All is not lost. What
is lost is the delusion that men can live by compromise
alone. This delusion is an empty and negative form of
extremism. It is nihilism—the heroic negation of the heroic

*Tragedy*

in life. If we were to follow it consistently, we should become zeroes and tempt others to take our places. The world of human nature abhors a vacuum. When some men shrink altogether from the heroic, others are tempted to use it in its worst form.

Finally, in order to act wisely we must free ourselves from the half-truths designed to prove that the justice of our individual fate depends upon our choice between moderation and heroic action. All universal meaning in tragic poetry depends upon our recognition that in respect to justice the fate of the tragic hero is the same as that of the moderate man. Nietzsche was wrong in assuming that life can be justified only by living intensely. On the other hand, it is the tender sentimentalist, never the hero himself, who shrinks from the grand reversals which turn life into drama and history; and Aristotle was right in recognizing the compensations of heroic deeds, even if that recognition does invalidate his general criticism of the tragic hero. The Ahabs and Lincolns, the Cordelias and Antigones, accept their fate because they know its inner reality, the exaltation which accompanies suffering or dying for principles. The death of the hero is an affirmation of the unalterable conditions of life, a memorable symbol for multitudes who show their own acceptance by living.

There is justice in life for both the hero and the moderate man. The very surface of events points to it. What the hero gains in intensity, he usually loses in duration. What the moderate man gains in duration, he usually loses in intensity. But there is a deeper reality which unites heroes and moderate men in a common destiny. Both are subject to the fixed conditions whereby sorrow is the price

148

of joy. Through the two-sided nature of human feeling, with its poles of good and evil, each pays for what he gets. The hero takes all, gives all, in one grand moment. The moderate man pays a little, lives to doze in his chair, and pays a little more. The choice between intensity and duration cannot upset the just equation whereby men pay with their lives for experience.

# VIII ✳

# The Tragic Spirit

# in Modern Times

WHAT is the tragic spirit? As an introduction to my answer, I shall quote two short poems on pain and suffering. The first is a translation from Sappho by W. S. Landor:

> Mother, I cannot mind my wheel;
> My fingers ache, my lips are dry;
> Oh! if you felt the pain I feel!
> But oh! who ever felt as I!

The second, entitled "The Mystery of Pain," is by Emily Dickinson:

> Pain has an element of blank;
> It cannot recollect
> When it began, or if there were
> A day when it was not.

It has no future but itself,
Its infinite realms contain
Its past, enlightened to perceive
New periods of pain.

One reason why these two lyrics are memorable is that they remind us of an important aspect of suffering and pain, namely, of the sufferer's loneliness, of his feeling of complete isolation from his fellows. Sappho's poem reveals the sufferer's craving for sympathetic understanding and his despairing conviction that no one else can understand because no one else has ever suffered as he suffers. When we read Sappho's poem in a carefree moment, we may smile a bit at human nature because we know the answer to the question. "But oh! who ever felt as I!" The answer is, of course, everyone—without exception. To an actual sufferer, however, we would, if we could, answer the question as convincingly and gently as possible. We would offer the consolation and relief that come to the sufferer who knows that his suffering is a meaningful bond uniting him with his fellows, and not a void separating him from them. Indeed, to answer the sufferer, we would, if we could, be tragic poets.

The second poem is more intellectual and possibly less touching, but it has the merit of turning into explicit statement the sufferer's sense that he is cut off, not only from his fellows, but also from the past and the future. "Pain," says Emily, "cannot recollect / When it began, or if there were / A day when it was not. / It has no future but itself."

For the sufferer who cannot escape from the insulated awareness of his own pain, there can be no significant pattern evident in the ever-flowing now of experience.

Living in a void without memory or hope, he cannot discover meaning or purpose in his being. Pain truly has an intensity which makes the sufferer forget its context, and experienced or considered by itself, it has a singleness, a uniqueness, which precludes intelligibility.

These two poems deserve to live, but neither has even the smallest place in the world's tragic literature. Lyric poetry is subjective and intensive: it is most effective when it does all that words can do to represent a single mood, feeling, or value. Tragic poetry is universal: at its best, it represents the sum total of all possible feelings, moods, and values. Sappho and Emily Dickinson deepen our understanding of suffering as a single, separate phenomenon, and of its power to cut us off from our fellow men and from the cosmos. Such a revelation of the nature of suffering is an indispensable part of tragic poetry, but it is only a part. Sophocles and Shakespeare show us the sufferings of individuals, but they achieve their tragic effects by presenting the individual sufferer as a representative of mankind and by showing us the justice which brings to every man equal measures of suffering and joy.

## I

Although Emily Dickinson wrote in the nineteenth century and Sappho more than twenty-five hundred years ago, their two poems seem quite modern in substance and spirit. Our own age—modern times—has thus far shown an acute awareness of pain as an isolated phenomenon, an awareness which characterizes its chief contributions in literature and criticism. Our modern world has been repeatedly described as a wasteland; our age is pleased to think of itself as peculiarly the Age of Anxiety; we have mourned over a lost generation; we have elaborated the theory that the artist is a sick man whose function is either to reveal his own frustration or to mirror faithfully the sufferings of a sick society.

These themes do not exhaust the wealth and variety of contemporary literature and criticism. Their supporters have, however, succeeded in making them seem to be the especially modern themes. One finds, therefore, in our climate of opinion a widespread assumption which reminds us of Sappho's "But oh! who ever felt as I!" and a resulting state of mind parallel to Emily Dickinson's observation that "pain . . . cannot recollect when it began" and "has no future but itself." The widespread assumption is that, because of his deep and unsoothed wounds, modern man is unique: other men in other times may have suffered as he has suffered, but they had remedies and consolations which we supposedly have lost. The resulting state of mind can be described as a kind of temporal provincialism. Believing himself unique, modern man is too often interested only in modern ideas and modern books, particularly those which faithfully portray his plight. He thinks of the great writers of the past as being great because they had something to say to the men of their own times, and not because they have something to say to him. He can appreciate only those writers who confirm his belief that modern man is unique.

Understandably enough, in an age preoccupied with suffering as a single, separate phenomenon, the words tragedy and tragic are commonly misused. To journalists tragedy is a synonym for disaster, calamity, or catastrophe, and tragic a synonym for disastrous, calamitous, and catastrophic. A flood washes away a dam; a drought brings on a famine; an airplane flight ends in a crash landing—such is the nature of tragedy and the tragic to modern journalists; the more unexpected, the more inexplicable the disaster, the greater is the tragedy. In common usage, then, the word tragic has acquired a meaning which is the exact opposite of the meaning it must have had for Aeschylus, who above all else sought to make suffering bearable by making it intelligible.

Modern reviewers, moreover, in applying the words tragedy and tragic to current books commonly have in mind the popular rather than the original usage; a book is profound and tragic if it shows an individual living a life without meaning, or if it portrays the disintegration of contemporary civilization, or if, in the eyes of the author or of his hero, reality is a chaos instead of a cosmos.

The masterpieces of Sophocles and Shakespeare represent disasters as sensational and shocking as any so-called tragedy in modern life: the misfortunes of Oedipus, who blinds himself in an agony of grief when he discovers that he has murdered his father and married his own mother, or of Othello, who kills himself when he discovers the innocence of Desdemona, would be reported, if they were actual events, under headlines on the front pages of most newspapers. In *Oedipus the King* and in *Othello,* however, we find much more than the meaningless evil which confronts us in the report of an actual disaster. The disaster which overtakes the Sophoclean or Shakespearean hero is not presented to us as a single, shocking fact, meaningless in its isolation from other facts, but as a link in an intelligible chain of events. This chain of events reveals links between the fate of the hero and his character and between his prosperity and his adversity, and it furnishes us with the evidence which enables us to find in the worst evils that can afflict men proof that in human affairs an intelligible order prevails.

## II

Since it is positive and affirmative, great tragic poetry satisfies our deepest rational and moral inclinations. As rational beings, we are always looking for patterns, for order, for meaning, in experience; as moral beings, we can be satisfied only by discovering in the realm of good and evil the special kind of pattern or order which we call justice. Tragedy reconciles us to evil by showing us that it is not a single, separate phenomenon but one side of change of fortune, and makes us feel that the change of fortune of a representative man is just.

Melodrama, it must be admitted, also satisfies our rational and moral nature: it too presents an order which is just. The inadequacy of melodrama arises from the fact that the just order which it represents will not stand the test of critical judgment. The first premise of melodrama distorts the facts of life. Men, we know, are neither angels nor devils. When we know only the good side of someone and know nothing of his weaknesses, we rightly think of him as being a bit too good for this world. And when, forgetting our better understanding of human nature, we think that someone has for his object in life a goal which he knows to be evil and evil only—as Mephistopheles has for his goal the downfall of Faust—we correctly think of him as diabolical. If such a person did live on earth, he would be a devil, not a man.

The conclusion of melodrama, which follows inescapably from its first premise, is also false to the facts as we know them. Poetic justice is more often the exception than the rule; indeed we call it "poetic" justice because we have found it oftener in literature than in life. Sometimes, it is true, the innocent are rewarded and the guilty punished; more often the innocent and the guilty escape together or are punished together, as in war; sometimes the innocent suffer while the guilty go free.

No one has ever questioned the superiority of tragedy over melodrama. All who have known and enjoyed both testify that tragedy is greater and more effective because it presents a more convincing picture of man and of the relation between his grief and his gladness.

Tragic insight offers us a mean between all melodramatic extremes—between the extremes of optimism and pessimism, between the extremes of fatalism and utopianism, and between the view that man is naturally good and the view that he is inherently depraved.

The tragic artist is neither optimist nor pessimist: he represents good and evil as eternally necessary aspects of experience, and the relation between them as just. Change of fortune is the condition of man's destiny on earth; no man can hope to be happy and happy only; no man need fear that he may sink into endless misery. To the tragic poet man is like the sunflower. It is the nature of the sunflower to turn toward the sun, but it is its destiny to live half in sunshine, half in shadow. Similarly, it is the nature of man to seek happiness, but it is his destiny to suffer as well as to enjoy.

Tragedy reminds the utopian that suffering and all forms of evil are always with us—that change of fortune is the fundamental and inevitable condition of our experience.

Whoever seeks to evade this inevitable condition merely hastens its fulfillment. Perhaps that is why, in an age dedicated to the task of bringing to all freedom from fear and insecurity, we are all so fearful and insecure. Certainly, by tragic irony, the utopian hopes of man are today closer to reversal than to realization.

On the other hand, tragedy reminds the fatalist that man can get what he wants—if he is willing to pay the price. Although he pays a heavy price for success, the tragic hero does reach his goal. Oedipus finds the unknown murderer; Orestes and Hamlet punish the murderers of their fathers; Medea crushes Jason; Tamburlaine conquers kingdoms and empires; Doctor Faustus has his four and twenty years, and Faust his fair moment; Romeo is united with Juliet in life and in death; Lear has ample proof of Cordelia's love, as does Othello of Desdemona's; Everyman is saved; Samson destroys the Philistines; Solness climbs the tower; Ahab hurls the harpoon at Moby Dick. Tragedy is not a spectacle of futility and frustration; it is a demonstration of the universal moral law: man gets what he pays for, and pays for what he gets.

The tragic view of man's moral capacities is again a mean between two extreme views. The tragic hero—the representative man—is neither eminently virtuous nor totally depraved. He has equal capacities for good and for evil; he is free to choose between a good deed and wrongdoing, and is responsible for his choice.

These are the main features of the tragic spirit. It lifts us above self-pity and reconciles us to suffering by showing that evil is a necessary part of the intelligible and just order of our experience. It lifts us above the divisive spirit of melodrama by showing that men are neither naturally good nor inherently evil. It saves us from the pitfalls of utopianism and fatalism. It teaches moderation by showing that the way of the extremist is short, but at the same time it shows the man of principle that an uncompromising stand is not without its just compensations. And most important, it teaches us that all men are united in the kinship of a common fate, that all are destined to suffer and enjoy, each according to his capacity.

### III

Since the tragic spirit lifts us out of the mood of disillusion, some of the tenets designed to preserve and justify this mood imply that in modern times the tragic vision is either an impossibility or itself an illusion.

The fact that we have produced no great contemporary tragedy—no picture of modern man which shows him as a glorious being, capable of reaching the heights and the depths and capable of discovering in his experience a meaning which justifies it—is proof, we have often been told, that the times are out of joint, that civilization is disintegrating, and that man in our age, in comparison with man in the great ages of Sophocles and Shakespeare, is enfeebled in spirit. The assumption behind this oft-repeated assertion seems to be that tragic poets in other ages have been able, without seeming to be ridiculous, to sketch their ideal tragic heroes from contemporary life. Is this true? Certainly not of the Greeks. The glorious company of Greek tragic heroes whom we know—Prometheus, Agamemnon, Orestes, Electra, Oedipus, Antigone, Medea, Hippolytus—were all legendary figures. Certainly it is not true of Shakespeare. His tragic heroes and plots are all drawn from the past, often the dim and legendary past—King Lear, Macbeth—and often from distant places —Caesar, Antony and Cleopatra, Romeo, Othello, Hamlet. Nor true of Marlowe—Tamburlaine, Doctor Faustus, Edward II. Nor of Milton—Samson Agonistes. Nor of Goethe—Faust. Nor of French classical tragedy. Indeed, not until we come to Ibsen do we find a dramatist who repeatedly attempts to demonstrate the conditions of our destiny with models drawn from contemporary life.

One reason why the poets have either consciously or instinctively turned to the past in their search for heroes suitable for tragedy is that, to be dramatically most effective, the hero must be a person of some consequence, and yet must be a man like ourselves, and neither eminently virtuous like the hero of melodrama, nor altogether vicious like the melodramatic villain. To find such a person in contemporary society in any age is indeed difficult, not because they do not exist but because we cannot view them without partisan bias. Men of consequence live in every age, and every man is a man like ourselves. But in a world of different factions, parties, sects, faiths, and nations, the contemporary hero in any age always has followers, who through partisanship are blind to his faults, and enemies, who are equally blind to his virtues. The saint is only a fool to the village atheist. And even after almost a century the birthday of Abraham Lincoln, who saved the American Union and freed the slaves, is ignored in the states which formed the vanquished Confederacy, which celebrate instead the birthdays of Jefferson Davis and of General Robert E. Lee.

Whether anyone has ever succeeded in writing a great tragedy with a contemporary hero is a matter of opinion. I have already praised *Moby Dick* as a tragic masterpiece.

## Tragedy

Ibsen's celebrated *Ghosts* presents a one-sided naturalistic picture rather than a tragedy; we see Oswald, never as a free and responsible man like ourselves but always as determined by past events, not as a man but as a mere ghost of the past. The plots of *Hedda Gabler* and *The Master Builder* are Sophoclean in their artful combinations of changes of fortune with reversals and discoveries, but their central figures are too cold and self-centered, too small-souled, to be fully acceptable as human beings like ourselves, a defect which can be attributed to Ibsen's limitations as an artist rather than to any loss in stature by modern man. Eugene O'Neill is more gifted with tragic insight than any other modern writer, and in *Beyond the Horizon* and *The Great God Brown* he has come close, and in *The Emperor Jones* even closer, to success in the attempt to invest figures drawn from contemporary life with tragic dignity. But although his best plays are poetic and tragic in other respects, their weakness in diction is a serious defect. Euripides is said to have been the most quoted writer in antiquity; Shakespeare has enriched the English language; but we never meet a man who can quote a line from O'Neill. Whether any other modern writer has succeeded in finding in contemporary life the model for a great tragic hero is also a matter of opinion. One point, however, is a matter of fact, not of opinion. It is not our age which alone has failed to write contemporary tragedy.

Further, the fact that our age has not produced an artist in tragedy to rival Sophocles and Shakespeare is no proof that the human spirit is becoming enfeebled. The thirteenth century and the eighteenth century were great ages, but they produced no rivals to Sophocles and Shakespeare. In every mountain range only a few peaks can stand out as highest; the best in every activity are, by definition, best because they are better than others; and they are necessarily rare. Between Sophocles and Shakespeare a period of some twenty-one hundred years elapsed; and since Shakespeare died only three hundred years ago, we can wait another eighteen hundred years before we need worry about the decline of the human spirit.

## IV

If we Americans search our civilization for an ideal tragic hero, we cannot find him in literature; we must turn to life itself, and even there we can find, I think, only one —Abraham Lincoln.

Lincoln had artistic gifts of the highest order and an unsurpassed comic and tragic insight into the absurdities and depths of human nature. His less-gifted contemporaries could never understand how the Lincoln of the droll stories and politically effective witticisms could be the same man as the author of the Gettysburg and Second Inaugural addresses. As Carl Sandburg brilliantly remarks, limited and conventional worthies could never understand "the wriggling in one human frame of Hamlet and Falstaff." In an older community Lincoln might well have become a great comic and tragic poet. The frontier drove him, as a matter of course, into public speaking and politics, the only arts it could afford. His mastery of the art of politics equaled that of Sophocles and of Shakespeare in the theatre.

As President, Lincoln consciously aimed to leave the nation a solemn reminder of its historic meaning, a testament of faith worthy of a place beside the Declaration of Independence. In the Gettysburg Address he succeeded. But he rightly regarded the Second Inaugural Address as his own best accomplishment. In it he reveals his full stature as a perfect tragic hero and views the terrible Civil War with supreme tragic insight.

The address was delivered in March, 1865, at the beginning of his second term as President and about six weeks before his death. At the time, victory for the North seemed to be in sight, but in an uncertain world, it was not certain.

Lincoln's Second Inaugural is in length only a wonderful soliloquy, filled with tragic insight, but the hero and the occasion give it adequate magnitude. In it the hero reveals all his qualities: his strength of purpose, his depth and breadth of feeling, his ability to penetrate to the central meaning of events. First, let us remember his unyielding will, the fundamental intensity of the hero. "With firmness in the right, as God gives us to see the right," he tells us, "let us strive on to finish the work we are in." The "work" he refers to is the prosecution of the war, at first fought to preserve the Union, and now, two years after his Emancipation Proclamation, being fought also to abolish African slavery. Next we should notice the depth and range of his feeling. Although he is himself the central actor in the drama, although he has been vilified and threatened with death, and although he is each day tormented by the necessity of making decisions which go against the grain of a kindly man, he gives no thought to himself except insofar as he is one of the people for whom he grieves. And the people for whom he grieves are not the people of the North alone: "this terrible war," "this mighty scourge of war," has been given to both North and

South. And finally, with his tragic insight, what does he see? Does he see only suffering—chance and meaningless? He sees a tragic justice in events—not a melodramatic justice, with deserved victory for virtuous Northerners and deserved defeat for vicious Southerners. He sees a nation, with all its people, North and South, a nation which in its Declaration of Independence had published its faith in human equality to all the world, punished for its failure to live up to its faith.

Fondly do we hope—fervently do we pray—that this mighty scourge of war may speedily pass away. Yet, if God wills that it continue until all the wealth piled by the bondsman's two hundred and fifty years of unrequited toil shall be sunk, and until every drop of blood drawn with the lash shall be paid by another drawn with the sword, as was said three thousand years ago, so still it must be said, "The judgments of the Lord are true and righteous altogether."

And with this vision of justice fulfilled through mutual suffering, he can look forward to reconciliation and peace.

With malice toward none; with charity for all; with firmness in the right, as God gives us to see the right, let us strive on to finish the work we are in; to bind up the nation's wounds; to care for him who shall have borne the battle and for his widow, and his orphan—to do all which may achieve and cherish a just and a lasting peace, among ourselves, and with all nations.

Here, for once, life outdoes art: not only Ahab, but even Oedipus and Hamlet are outmatched. But no, on second thought, art had its share in the shaping of this hero and this occasion. Abraham Lincoln was himself a supreme artist. As a self-made man, through fidelity to principle he shaped himself into the ideal hero; and if we

see in the great Civil War a step in the moral perfection
of man rather than a meaningless collision of forces, we
are, first of all, indebted to his fidelity to principle and
to his tragic vision.

## V

On a world-wide scale, this age is like the age of Abraham Lincoln, who said in 1858, three years before the
Civil War:

"A house divided against itself cannot stand." I believe this
government cannot endure permanently half slave and half
free. I do not expect the Union to be dissolved—I do not expect the house to fall—but I do expect it will cease to be divided. It will become all one thing, or all the other.

His words proved to be altogether prophetic; and it may
well be that they foretell the course of events in a world
divided now between freedom and slavery, just as they
foretold the course of events in the United States a hundred years ago.

Our age is neither better nor worse than any other age.
The life of man—caught, like the heart of Gloucester,
" 'twixt two extremes of passion, joy and grief," and often
"alack! too weak the conflict to support"—is always
tragic, in all times and all places. But this age, the age of
the World Wars, is different from other and more serene
ages in the degree of its intensity. It is a heroic age. Like
the whalers on the *Pequod*, we are carried away by the
iron will of the Ahabs who propose either to make us
swallow their prescriptions or to liquidate us. Like Abraham Lincoln, the ordinary man in modern times is often
obliged, against his desires, to be an extremist—to play

the part of a tragic hero. As tragedy shows us, the conditions of human destiny are universal, and justice prevails in the lives of ordinary men as it prevails in the lives of heroes; but men should have the choice between the heroic and the ordinary, between intensity and duration. We, who would choose the little ups and downs of peace, are in danger of having war with its spectacular changes of fortune thrust upon us.

Like Abraham Lincoln, "fondly do we hope" that the world will become all free, and that freedom will come through the triumph of wisdom on both sides rather than through the judgment of war. If we are to realize our hopes, we need all the understanding and patience which tragic insight can furnish. We cannot meet the challenge of the times if we are sunk in a mood of disillusion and self-pity. We need to be lifted above the melodramatic mood which the spirit of war has brought, with the aid of demagogues, into our politics and our daily lives. Much as we disagree with their principles and condemn their methods, we must always see the people on the other side of any question, at home or abroad, not as melodramatic villains, but as men like ourselves, who seek the good as they see it, even though their clouded judgment and passions may bring about their downfall and involve us in their ruin.

And if war comes, as it came for Abraham Lincoln—if we are driven against our desires, as he was driven against his desires, to defend with the sword the union of free states and the dignity and freedom of the individual human being—then we shall have even greater need for the tragic wisdom which can find the significance of terrible events, which can assure us that fidelity to duty has its rewards, and which alone can use the common suffering of both sides in war as the means to their eventual understanding and reconciliation.

For the tragic spirit was the highest achievement of Athenian democracy; through Abraham Lincoln it ennobled this Republic at the time of its first great trial; and it alone can bring about that union of hearts which Alexander the Great once prayed for as a means of uniting Macedonians and Persians, and which must come if ever the sharers of a common fate are to be united in a world-wide society.

## VI

In modern times we are reaching the end of a long period during which an optimistic faith in progress-to-happiness on earth has prevailed. The popular faith in progress was a great illusion; many good things, it must be admitted, came from it; and in spite of the sufferings of modern man in war and revolution—in spite of the tragic reversal whereby we seem more likely to turn earth into a hell than into a heaven—the old illusion dies hard. As both statesmen and demagogues know, many men in modern times, as yet unable to find a satisfactory substitute, still cling to the old popular faith.

Until recently our age has been too much under the spell of the great illusion of progress to discover the tragic vision. Our age has been too busy in its search for joy-without-sorrow to spare more than an occasional Melville to tell our tragic story, and too busy to heed it when it is told.

The ablest of our poets and critics have discovered the inadequacies of this faith and, in trying to come to terms with the stubborn fact that evil is an ever-present aspect of experience, have reached at least a partial understanding of the meaning of tragedy. The American critic, F. O. Matthiessen, for example, stressed the development of tragic insight from Baudelaire to Yeats and Eliot, showing the reaction by critics and poets against a groundless optimism and ending in the beginnings of tragic insight.

But the majority of writers and critics who have lost the popular faith in progress-to-happiness on earth have found nothing to replace it; they think of suffering as a single, separate phenomenon, and of modern man as unique, or almost unique, in his sufferings; they have lost the great illusion only to lapse into an empty and negative state of disillusion. Disillusion is the most overworked word in modern writing, both critical and creative, so that two forms of the word are needed to carry the burden. Some prefer disillusion; others prefer disillusionment, which may be a stronger form, meaning complete, permanent, and militant disillusion.

Since we have all lost some illusion, we can sympathize with the mood of disillusion. And since we have all suffered, we know that it is human—all too human—for the sufferer to cry out, "But oh! who ever felt as I," and to feel cut off from his fellow men, past, present, and future. But in modern times we have witnessed the hardening of the mood of disillusion into a creed, with tenets which have, after thirty years of overuse, become venerable clichés.

Because the creed of disillusion is only a rationalization intended to justify this hardening of an understandable temporary mood into a permanent attitude toward life, the arguments supporting its tenets are certain to be merely specious. Their disproof is not enough, however, to cure the ailment. Disillusion is an emotional as well as an intellectual state of being: what is needed is a view of life which touches the feelings as well as the mind and which has the power to lift the viewer out of the narrow swamp of self-pity and on to the broad and healthy plains of a sympathy directed toward all men. What is needed is a remedy which will first make the disillusioned soul see and feel, as Matthiessen, Eliot, and Yeats have seen and felt, that "there is no such thing as good unless there is also evil, or evil unless there is good" and which at last will make him see and feel, as Sophocles and Shakespeare have seen and felt, that the rise and fall of a representative man is the symbol of a justice which universally prevails.

Tragic poetry, with its magnificent appeal to both feelings and mind, has this power—if we take it seriously. And why should we not take seriously an art which has brought deep satisfaction to many generations of audiences and readers, and which has never failed to win from perceptive and intelligent critics the tribute which belongs to the highest of the arts—the art which best reveals the full possibilities of human insight?

We can understand why anyone under the spell of the great illusion of progress must reject the tragic vision. As views of life, utopianism and tragic wisdom are incompatible. But the disillusioned soul—he who has lost faith in romantic optimism—is seemingly well prepared for the realism of the tragic poet, who through his courageous recognition of the worst succeeds in showing that the worst is the counterpart and proof of the best.

Here, however, we come upon the deepest resistance of the disillusioned soul to a disturbance of his mood and upon the tenet of his creed which is most difficult to answer. All visions of order and justice in the universe, he maintains, are illusions. Tragedy is realistic when it is seen only as a spectacle of suffering, but when we derive from it a sense of reconciliation, we are being lulled by a splendidly effective trick, whereby the artist imposes his own sense of form on the formless.

This argument, if valid, cuts both ways: if we apply it to the tragic poets, we must also apply it to the prophets of disillusion. For if all creative pictures of life are merely subjective, does it not follow that the disillusioned writer's picture of life is not, as his admiring reviewers maintain, a faithful mirroring of the inevitable frustration of man in a disintegrating society and a meaningless universe, but only a faithful mirroring of the futility of his own emotional attitude and of the chaos and incoherence of his own mind?

If such is the nature of creative art—if men are altogether cut off from knowledge of the meaning of human values and must live together by the flickering light of opinions dictated by different temperaments and intellectual capacities—whose company shall we prefer, whose light shall we choose? The tragic poet's or the disillusioned writer's? The disillusioned writer tempts us to indulge in self-pity by confirming the defeatism of those dark moments in which we can find neither rhyme nor reason in events; the tragic poet encourages us to drown self-pity in universal sympathy. If we were confronted with a choice on these terms, I think we would say, "All honor to the tragic poet, who reminds us of the best that is in us, even if he cannot prove to us that his vision is the order of the universe."

Does life itself provide the pattern for tragedy, or is

life itself, apart from the tragic artist's vision, formless and unintelligible? Are change of fortune, reversal, discovery, irony, and incidents in a necessary sequence faithful reproductions of the fundamental forms of experience, or are they merely artistic inventions, whereby the tragic poet imposes his own sense of form upon the formless, his own meaning upon the meaningless, his own vision of order and justice upon chance and chaos?

Aristotle believed that the poet finds his forms and patterns in life itself: "Tragedy," he said, "is an imitation of an action." Furthermore, he believed that the poet discovers universal forms and patterns: "Poetry," he said, "is higher and more philosophical than history, for poetry stresses the universal, whereas history stresses the particular." Others have disagreed with Aristotle. Nietzsche reached the conclusion, derived partly from Schopenhauer's pessimism, partly from his own study of Greek tragedy, that only as an aesthetic phenomenon is life eternally justified.

Although we have seen in the past few years a growing appreciation of the tragic spirit and vision, and although we may live to see a great new age of poetic and tragic drama, we must assume that our contemporaries who feel isolated from their fellow men, and from the past and the future, find in tragedy at best only an effective artistic illusion, and not an accurate description of the life of man in modern times.

I cannot agree either with Nietzsche, or with our contemporaries who believe that the tragic view of life is at best an illusion. I agree with Aristotle that the tragic poet finds his forms and patterns in life itself, in experiences common to all; and since I do not share Aristotle's desire to exclude the poets from the realm of reason, I find in tragic poetry the important view of life which he ignored.

Without appealing to supernatural faith—an appeal which the disillusioned writer would reject—I think it can be shown that the tragic poet's vision, though limited, is real and not an illusion, and that the great scientist and the great tragic poet are equally reliable reporters—one of the events in the physical world, the other of man's joys and sorrows, his change of fortune. Tragic poetry is not the only source of wisdom concerning values, nor can it provide us, on many important points, with more than fancies something like the truth, but the tragic view of life is something more than a splendid illusion, and it still has the power, if properly appreciated, to deprive pain of some of the sharp edges which Sappho and Emily Dickinson describe.

## ❧ PART FOUR

# *On Insight and Objectivity*

# IX ❧

# Tragic Poetry and Science

SINCE the teacher of English serves his school and his community by imparting the skill in reading and writing necessary in the study of the other arts and sciences, he is thoroughly familiar with the use of his subject as a means to other ends. Yet, however pressed he may be in the service of others, he never doubts that literature should be taught primarily as an end in itself. He feels that literature has significance as an independent subject because it has been important to him, but he is seldom prepared, as are the teachers of the natural and social sciences, to explain to others clearly the intrinsic values of his material. If he sets out seriously to consider whether the study of literature has a value independent of the mere training in reading which will enable the student to grasp the great truths of science, he first runs into the question whether any science or art can remain independent in an ideal curriculum.

There are many who feel that some one art or science is so important that all others must be subordinated to it. This kind of enthusiasm for a new subject, or for a new aspect of an old one, always seems novel and advanced, although it is a very old phenomenon in the world of learning, and reformers who from time to time would subordinate literature or other subjects to some supposedly higher kind of knowledge think they are advancing the cause of education. With that opinion I cannot agree. The theory that the arts and sciences must be arranged in an order of importance, from lowest to highest, is neither new nor progressive. It is, on the contrary, a new form of the old *scala perfectionis,* the ladder of perfection on which the scholar ascended from the lowest profane science to the highest reaches of theology, just as the saintly mystic climbed, rung by rung, the levels of being leading to ultimate union with the divine.

This old theory [1] that all arts and sciences are handmaidens to one supreme system of truths can be put into practice only when all can agree upon a theology that can be used as the highest rung in the ladder. Such a theology we no longer have in common. Some find a "theology" in a scientific or mathematical mysticism; others find one in the residuum from the vapors of the social sciences; still others come to rest in a kind of hypnosis induced by dialectics and doctrinaire economics. As the latest "theologies" of Freud, Spengler, Pareto, and a swarm of lesser

---

[1] For a detailed treatment of this subject, see H. A. Myers, "Scholasticism in Modern Thought," *Journal of Philosophy*, March, 1939.

lights rise and fall in the heavens, their exponents expect us to follow the world-view of the year by means of the book of the month, the thought of the week, and the five new words of the day. When the latest of these systems of truth stands the test of a single generation or of a single decade, then we may consider the possibility of subordinating other arts and sciences to it.

It is not difficult to show that the old ladder of perfection in many respects still reigns supreme as an index forced upon experience. Many of our thinkers wander about between the divided worlds of the subjective and the objective, pondering how to make one truth out of two; others perpetually arrange and rearrange the entities and constructs of the sciences into imaginary levels of worth or reality; still others approach reality armed with categories that are merely synonyms for old ways of thinking. If historians have drawn us a picture of the medieval philosopher, pitiful in his subservience to theology, we can draw an equally accurate picture of the modern thinker who is subservient to the theology of "scientific method." For him philosophy is handmaiden to mathematics and the natural sciences, and the function of the philosopher is to play the sedulous ape to these disciplines.

A philosophical legend concerning the nature of truth has grown up in modern thought which teaches that objective things are true and that subjective things are the source of error and falsity. This legend is the exact counterpart of the eternal and temporal worlds of the schoolmen and their consequent possibility of a theory of twofold truth. The Greeks were unaware of the distinction between the subjective and the objective; and modern

thinkers are apparently unaware that the distinction is
not a real division, that it is the result of a distinction
between orders of thought and not a separation between
things thought and *things experienced but free from the
alleged infirmities of thought.* It has taken many modern
experiments to determine what ought to be obvious,
namely, that the so-called objective order is a thought-
construct of exactly the same standing with respect to
truth as the subjective.

From the subjective considered as a system impersonal
in its nature I distinguish the personal perspective, the
private biography of the individual. Modern thinkers have
often confused the two. They think that knowledge is
made valid and ideas adequate by escaping from subjectivity to objectivity. In this way they approach but
confuse the truth, which is that ideas are made adequate
by changing from a personal to an impersonal perspective.
A subjective system, *if it is communicable,* is impersonal
and adequate.

The fault lies in failing to distinguish between subjectivity as an impersonal system or perspective and the
private personal point of view of the individual. With this
distinction in mind, the process of making knowledge a
matter of truth and meaning does not consist in getting
knowledge out of the subjective system and into the objective system; it consists in *systematizing* knowledge, in
putting the experience of the private person in impersonal
systems. In this sense, true objectivity can be acquired in
a system of subjectivity ("The world is my idea") as completely as it can be acquired in a system of objectivity.

For nearly five hundred years the truly progressive
view of the arts and sciences has been that they approach

experience, each by an independent road, as the spokes of a wheel come to a common center in the hub.[1] This view does not contradict the unity of human experience. There is as much unity in the modern picture of knowledge as a great wheel in which every spoke leads directly to the hub as there is in the medieval view of knowledge as a ladder on which no step except the highest leads directly to truth and the good life. Each view stresses the unity of knowledge, but there is an important difference between the modern wheel and the medieval ladder. According to the medieval view, one step—literature, for example—merely leads to a higher step; according to the modern view, literature has independent and enduring worth because it leads us in its own way directly to the inner meaning of events.

The case for literature as an independent subject in the curriculum must rest, I believe, on the proof that literature has its own important way of leading us to the very center of things and that it is not merely a lower step in the ladder of knowledge, useful only in leading to higher kinds of thought. All of us who teach English contribute to this proof by our faith in the intrinsic worth of literature. Beyond that it is not necessary that we see eye to eye. I wish to swell the chorus of our common faith by voicing my own belief that tragic poetry has the same worth, as a source of knowledge about values, as pure science has as a source of knowledge about nature. We can begin to teach our generation respect for insight by showing the devotees of objectivity that literature at its

[1] For the historical background and metaphysical implications of this theory, see H. A. Myers, *The Spinoza-Hegel Paradox: A Study of the Choice between Traditional Idealism and Systematic Pluralism* (Ithaca, N.Y.: Cornell University Press, 1944).

best, as in tragic poetry, possesses qualities similar to those which we admire in science at its best.

## II

If the distinguishing marks of science are accurate observation, compression, expression by means of a special language, and demonstration, then tragic poetry is remarkably like science in all these respects, for it is a shorthand account of fortune and misfortune, prepared by the most talented observers and presented in a language that is concise and to the point.

Poetry and science are alike in that each rests on observation, and especially on the kind of genius for observation which finds in the particular an instance of the universal. We all see the phenomena of nature every day but only a Copernicus suspects that the earth moves, only a Newton finds a law that governs falling bodies, only a Darwin finds a principle in ceaseless growth and change. Similarly, although the ups and downs of fortune and misfortune are the framework of our daily lives, only the tragic poet finds in change of fortune the meaning of our destiny. He alone discovers the just order which links good to evil. Science springs from careful observation, tragic poetry from insight.

As a shorthand account of experience, tragic poetry does not suffer by comparison with pure science. Both aim at the essence rather than at the details of life and nature. If the periodic table reduces all nature to a concise formula, *King Lear* compresses life to two hours' traffic on the stage. Newton's *Principia* is to bodies as Milton's *Samson* is to the spirit. Michelson and Morley throw light on physical measuring rods by means of a crucial experiment; Marlowe in *Tamburlaine* tests tragedy as a measuring rod for the will, and Shakespeare in *Othello* tests it as a measuring rod for the feelings. *Ars longa, vita brevis?* No, it is life that is too long to grasp; great science and great poetry are short and to the point.

Again, if the scientist finds in mathematics the only language which can faithfully describe the physical world as he sees it, the tragic artist finds in poetry the exact and adequate language of human values. These special languages, mathematics and poetry, have much in common.[1] In its highest reaches mathematics is a kind of scientific poetry which can describe

> The wondrous architecture of the world,
> And measure every wandering planet's course,
> Still climbing after knowledge infinite;

and great tragic poetry, the perfect language of joy and sorrow, is as convincing as a mathematical demonstration.

Seeing is believing. We believe the scientist because he can show us, by experiments and demonstrations, that his laws and principles accurately describe things as they are. We believe the tragic poet for the same reason. "Before he dies," says Sophocles, "count no man happy only"; and as a demonstration, he shows us the fall into misery of Oedipus, the great king who answered the riddle of the Sphinx and who may have seemed on the morning of his downfall to be happy only.

When we see that a tragedy is a kind of demonstration, the remarkable parallel between science and tragic poetry

[1] For further discussion of this point, see H. A. Myers, "The Usefulness of Figurative Language," *Quarterly Journal of Speech*, April, 1940.

is complete—each is a demonstration of principles or laws derived from experience by penetrating observation, and presented in compressed form, and in a special language.

The similarities between poetry and science should not, however, be used to support the mistaken belief that poetry is merely a feeble forerunner of science. It is as foolish today for the scientist to try to take the place of the poet as it once was for the poet to try to take the place of the scientist. Here, for example, are two glimpses of nature through the eyes of Heraclitus, the poet and philosopher who sneered at the early mathematicians and scientists. "This world," he says, "which is the same for all, no one of gods or man has made; but it was ever, is now, and ever shall be an everliving fire, with measures of its kindling and measures going out." That, I take it, is about all he had to offer as poetic physicist and chemist. Equally interesting and limited is the Heraclitean astronomy. A new sun, he thinks, is born each morning, only to die in the western waters at evening. Each sun must follow a fixed course: "Even the sun," he tells us, "must obey his measures, or the messengers of justice will find him out." Admittedly, Heraclitus is brilliant in one respect. The poet has a vision of order, and he finds order in nature. But Heraclitus also shows us the limitations of the poet when he tries to explain the physical world. The proper realm of the poet is human nature and human values; when he turns to the physical world, he cannot view it impersonally: he peoples it with living causes and poetic beings, endows atoms with human values, and guides the stars by means of messengers of justice.

Science is equally limited when it seeks to replace

poetry. The human spirit cannot be described by the impersonal categories of the sciences, just as the physical world cannot be adequately described from the personal point of view of the poet.

The life of man, if seen through the eyes of science only, is a cold and dreary business. "The life of man," says Bertrand Russell, the mathematician who was philosophizing about life as it is seen only from the impersonal point of view of science, "is a long march through the night, surrounded by invisible foes, tortured by weariness and pain, toward a goal that few can hope to reach, and where none may tarry long." As for man himself, "His origin, his growth, his hopes and fears, his loves and beliefs, are but the outcome of accidental collocations of atoms." He is doomed to live in "an alien and inhuman world." These dreary thoughts, which link the destiny of the individual human being to the death of the solar system, would frighten us if they adequately described our experience. But this is the world of science, not the world of experience. The world—all of it, including man and nature—is too large for science alone and too large for poetry alone, and indeed is a bit too large for both.

We turn to science with confidence for a description of the physical world, and we should turn with equal confidence to poetry for an understanding of values. We have every reason to believe that the forms (or categories) of tragic poetry—change of fortune, reversal, discovery, irony, necessary sequence of events, freedom of choice— are the fundamental forms of human experience, and that the tragic poet's revelation of a just relation between good and evil in the life of a representative man, tested and proved by many demonstrations, before generations of perceptive and intelligent witnesses, is real and not an illusion.

If these inferences are correct, then, science and poetry are parallel and independent roads to important truths about nature and life; one does not merely lead to the other; one cannot replace the other. Each leads in its own way to the center of experience. I offer as further support of my thesis the axioms concerning values that I find written boldly in tragedy.

*The life of feeling is never one-sided.*

*Men differ in degree, not in kind.*

*A man's character is his fate.*

*In the life of the spirit men get what they pay for, pay for what they get.*

Thus, in proportion to his capacity to feel, is each actor in the human drama brought to the extremes of joy and grief; in this manner each pays and is repaid for joy and grief in accordance with a law within himself—a law not to be found in Russell, not to be found in Einstein, not to be found in the vast extent of modern science.

### III

In the modern world the realm of knowledge, with its unlimited number of arts and sciences, should be viewed not as a kingdom with countless noisy claimants to the throne but as a republic in which each individual system is granted equal opportunity to reveal its own direct approach to truth. In respect to the arrangement of the arts and sciences I urge the adoption of intellectual democracy in place of an outworn intellectual feudalism.

But in a community of equal and independent arts and

sciences equal rights imply equal duties. Either literature
fits into the college curriculum because it is an independent road to truth or it does not belong in the curriculum at all. The teacher of literature who believes that
it belongs in the curriculum is committed at all times to
the task of justifying its presence. In his own manner he
must make literature lead directly to the center of experience, and not merely to the latest kind of higher learning;
directly to the man himself, and not vaguely to some
notion of good citizenship. There are doubtless many ways
of showing this independent significance. In discussing
the remarkable parallel between tragic poetry, the source
of wisdom about values, and science, the source of knowledge about nature, I have not meant to imply that this
method is either the only one or the best.

# X ✴

# Literature, Science,

# and Democracy

AT CORNELL University, where the College of
Agriculture maintains an Extension Bulletin Service which
furnishes New Yorkers with pamphlets on a great variety
of practical subjects, a professor of literature is often re-
minded that many people call *any* valuable piece of
writing literature. One letter which we received recently
will serve as a fair example of many. It was addressed to
the Department of Literature, Cornell University, but it
was clear from the contents that it was intended for the
Extension Bulletin Service, which the writer obviously
regarded as the center of literary activity at Cornell.
"Dear Sirs," he wrote. "Will you please send me as soon
as possible your latest literature on how to make sauerkraut?"

*186*

## And Democracy

What is the essential difference between literature and
other kinds of writing? Dictionaries still label as a col-
loquialism the use of the word literature to describe such
current printed matter as advertising circulars, income
tax directions, and college announcements, but the dic-
tionary definition of literature as "the total of the preserved writings belonging to a given language or people"
would certainly include a time-tested treatise on how to
make sauerkraut, and would seem also to include old
handbills or any kind of printed matter venerable enough
to be called "preserved." In recent years the editors who
compile anthologies for the use of students of American
literature have confirmed popular usage by leaning more
and more toward the broadest possible definition. A
recent anthology, for example, subtitled "Selections from
the Literature of the United States," includes in its offer-
ings passages from John Smith's *Description of New England,* Noah Webster's *Grammatical Institute of the English
Language,* Alexander Hamilton's *Report on Manufactures,*
Andrew Carnegie's *Empire of Business,* and Mr. Justice
Field's concurring opinion in the Slaughter-House Cases
of 1884.

In textbooks designed to show the growth of the American mind, or of American civilization, the selection of a
wide variety of writings is defensible, and even desirable,
but the literary critics and historians who confirm loose
popular usage by including purely impersonal, factual,
informative, and descriptive writings under the heading
of literature make doubly necessary a reconsideration of
what we mean when we speak of literature in its narrower

*187*

sense as one of the humanities, in the narrower sense which includes only such writings as *Oedipus the King,* or *Hamlet,* or *Moby Dick.*

The traditional distinction between the supposedly purely aesthetic values of belles-lettres and the informational and utilitarian values of other kinds of writing is vague and misleading. Everyone understands what is meant by informational and utilitarian values, but what is meant by purely aesthetic values? If the traditional definition of belles-lettres is understood to mean that the reading of poems, plays, novels, and essays is, generally speaking, a pleasurable experience, it affirms an undeniable fact, but it seems also to imply that literature in the narrow sense is valuable only because it offers recreation, diversion, and even escape from the actualities of a practical and troubled world. In the United States amusements have always been considered a matter more of private than of public concern, and the traditional identification of belles-lettres with purely aesthetic values may explain why the federal and state governments have done so little to encourage creative artists and why, for example, Cornell's Extension Bulletin Service is cheerfully supported by the taxpayers of New York State while its program in literature is dependent upon tuition payments and income from endowments.

Inherited from aristocratic theorists, the distinction between writings that afford aesthetic pleasures and writings that serve useful purposes is misleading on both sides, and is particularly unlikely to attract the citizens of a democratic society to the serious study of literature. On one side, this traditional distinction, contrary to the evidence, implies that writings intended primarily to be informative and useful are necessarily lacking in aesthetic qualities. On the other side, and worse, the distinction implies that great literature is neither informative nor useful. Nothing could be farther from the truth.

A cookbook or a textbook may have aesthetic qualities; a mathematical or scientific demonstration may be a thing of beauty; and *King Lear,* properly read, may be as informative and as useful as a treatise on sauerkraut.

The true difference between literature and other kinds of writing is indicated by the simple, but often forgotten, fact that there are two fundamentally different views of life, two ways of looking at man and the universe, one from within, the other from the outside. These views are equally valuable and indispensable: a culture or a civilization which glorifies one view and belittles the other is out of balance and in danger.

The first view is personal and insighted. This view is more than anthropocentric; it places each individual at the center of the universe and makes it possible for him to say, as Schopenhauer said: "The world is my idea."

From the individual's own point of view, the world begins and ends with his awareness of it. As long as he clings to this point of view, and believes in its validity, man is at home in the universe. As he sees the world from his personal, insighted point of view, it is a world of values: of pleasure and pain, of joy and sorrow, of beauty and ugliness, of victory and defeat, of success and failure, of good deeds and bad deeds, of rewards and punishments, of satisfaction and remorse.

In its beginnings this personal, insighted view is the simple awareness of the individual human consciousness, but in its highest reaches it is the vision, the poetic insight, of the artist who sees other people as he sees himself, from within, and who strengthens the bonds of society by demonstrating that the inner world of one individual is in its basic conditions the same as the inner world of another.

The second view is impersonal and external: it had its beginnings in the invention of the weights, measures, scales, clocks, thermometers, and calendars which make impersonal and external description possible. In turn external, impersonal description makes possible a variety of writings, ranging from almanacs and encyclopedias through scholarly monographs on literary history and on to the chemist's periodic table and Newton's *Principia.*

When man sees himself from within and the world as his world, he is the measure of all things; when he insists upon viewing himself from the outside only, he discovers that he is no longer the measure of anything.

What, then, is the indispensable quality, the distinguishing trait, of literature? What essential characteristic distinguishes the *Oresteia* from Aristotle's *Poetics, King Lear* from the footnotes in a scholarly edition, Whitman's *Leaves of Grass* from a treatise on the care of lawns?

My genial and talented colleague at Cornell, Professor Morris Bishop, once wrote a book of light verse which carried on its cover the title, *Paramount Poems,* followed by the assertion: "If it isn't a Paramount, it isn't a Poem."

Although negative in form, this is the shortest and clearest definition of poetry that I have ever seen. In the interest of clarity I propose now to offer first a definition of literature in similar negative form. My sentence is much longer than Morris Bishop's because it is much less exclusive.

If it doesn't open up for you the inner life of at least

one other human being, who may be either the author or one of his fictional creations; if it doesn't release you for a moment from your lonely island in the sea of the individual's isolation; if it doesn't inform you of some of the resources of the human spirit, of its triumphs and frustrations, or of its complexities, perversities, and incongruities; if it doesn't convince you that the inner world of the human spirit is as boundless and wonderful as the outer world of the seven seas and the starry heavens; if it doesn't indicate that the moral law is as important as the laws of thermodynamics; if it doesn't lead you toward an insighted understanding that, in spite of all outward and measurable differences, inwardly all human beings are akin—if it affects you in none of these ways, then no matter how great its other merits of diction and form and style may be, what you have been reading is not literature.

And now to turn this into positive form:

Other qualities of poetry and literary prose are important, but insight—the writer's personal view and his ability to see others as he sees himself, from within, his ability to estimate those inner values which cannot be checked by measuring rods, weights, clocks, and thermometers—is the indispensable quality, the distinguishing trait, of literature. Literature may offer more than insight, but it cannot offer less; it cannot lack insight without becoming another kind of writing. Literature without insight is a contradiction in terms.

## II

If the writer's personal, insighted view of life is the essential characteristic of all literature, how shall we distinguish major literary works from minor works? How shall we distinguish *Moby Dick* from "Annabel Lee," Milton's *Paradise Lost* from his sonnet on his blindness, *Murder in the Cathedral* from "The Love Song of J. Alfred Prufrock"?

One difference is that a major work has the adequate magnitude which a minor work lacks. An epic outweighs an epigram; the story of Tom Thumb lacks tragic dimensions; and Melville was right in choosing a whale rather than a flea for the subject of his masterwork. But magnitude alone cannot explain the difference between major and minor literary works. The grandeur of the theme of Joel Barlow's *Columbiad* and the length of the poem do not add up to a great work of art; Poe's "Raven" would be a minor poem even if it contained ten thousand lines instead of one hundred.

The main difference between minor and major literary works is that the minor work introduces us only to the writer's private personal world while the major work leads us into a world which, though it is not impersonal and dehumanized as is the world seen from the outside only, is nevertheless a world common to all. The more we read of Poe's poems and tales, the more we know about the private world of Edgar Allan Poe. Shakespeare's plays, in contrast, tell us very little about Shakespeare and very much about the world of human nature which we all share.[1]

In a major literary work—in *Leaves of Grass* or in *Moby Dick*—something is added to the writer's private point of view and world.

---

[1] For a discussion of expressionism, pseudoclassicism, and the grand style, see H. A. Myers, "Style and the Man," *South Atlantic Quarterly*, July, 1941.

1. The writer's insight is extended by sympathetic identification with others until he sees others as he sees himself. He then can offer us universality in addition to particularity or individuality. The very first line of the first edition of Whitman's *Leaves of Grass*—"I celebrate my-self"—promises us insight into the inner life of one individual human being. If *Leaves of Grass* offered us no more than the inner world of

Walt Whitman, a kosmos, of Manhattan the son,
Turbulent, fleshy, sensual, eating, drinking and breeding;
No sentimentalist, no stander above men and women or
    apart from them;
No more modest than immodest,

it would still be literature. It would even be great of its kind, but the kind would be minor.

The second and third lines of *Leaves of Grass,* however, promise us more than self-revelation. "And what I assume you shall assume," Walt goes on to say. "For every atom belonging to me as good belongs to you." Throughout *Leaves of Grass,* from the opening lines to the closing lines, Whitman identifies himself with others, with an imaginative sympathy which has rarely been equaled and never surpassed. "I do not ask the wounded person how he feels," he exclaims,

                    I myself become the wounded person;
My hurts turn livid upon me as I lean on a cane and
    observe.

I am the mash'd fireman with breast-bone broken. . . .

I am the hounded slave, I wince at the bite of the
    dogs. . . .

The disdain and calmness of martyrs, . . .
All these I feel or am.

Through insight into others Whitman reaches universality: he shows us not only the particular nature of one
man, Walt Whitman, but the common nature of man. He
leads us into a world common to all, in which we see all
men as equals and brothers who share a common fate.
That is why *Leaves of Grass,* with all its blemishes in
diction and form, is a major work of art while many
polished and nearly flawless poems are merely minor.

2. In tragedy, which many regard as the highest form of
literature, the artist offers us detachment as well as insight.

First of all, the artist in drama or fiction offers us insight. If he wishes to make his fictional personages seem
real to us and capable of affecting us as intensely as living
human beings affect us, he must identify himself with his
creatures, live their lives for them, and see the world as
they would see it. If he succeeds in doing this, he enables
us in turn, as spectators and readers, to identify ourselves
sympathetically with his fictional personages. Our insight
depends upon the artist's insight.

To create fictional personages who seem real to us, who
can affect us as living personages affect us, is a great
achievement of artistic insight. The lesser artist is content
to offer us no more. Satisfied with his power to engage our
sympathy, he offers us no more than the happy ending of
romantic fiction. He permits his Romeo to be reunited
with Juliet and to live happily ever after, his Hamlet to
avenge his father and rule over the kingdom, his Othello
to discover his mistake in time, his Macbeth to save himself through repentance, his Captain Ahab to kill the white
whale and return in triumph with an unusually large

cargo of whale oil. Thus, he satisfies our desire to see those with whom we identify ourselves sympathetically turn out well and find the happiness they seek.

The minor artist can provide us with a happy ending because, as a creator of fictional personages, he enjoys a kind of omnipotence. He is lord of his little fictional universe. But he can exercise his omnipotence only at the cost of failing to satisfy our critical intelligence. Although a happy ending satisfies our sympathetic interest in fictional personages, we know at once when we see it that we have been watching events in a dream world, where the artist as creator is omnipotent, and not events in the world common to all, in which even the insighted artist must bow to necessity.

The major artist, the tragic realist who wishes to present the world common to all rather than a dream world, must temper his insight with detachment. Once he has created a fictional personage with a definite character or moral bent—a Romeo, a Hamlet, an Othello, a Captain Ahab— that character or moral bent becomes an antecedent from which certain consequences inevitably follow. The tragic realist cannot save his hero from the consequences of character, nor does he attempt to do so. He cannot rescue his hero from the universal tragic predicament of human beings, nor does he attempt to do so. The best he can do for his hero is to grant him (and us as spectators or readers) a flash of insight into the meaning of human destiny, an insight which reconciles him to his fate. At the end Captain Ahab must die, but he accepts his fate, content to be what he is. And we, as we view with insight the full unfolding of the inevitable consequences of individual character and of universal human nature, are content to be what we are, human beings who share a common fate which is both terrible and glorious.

## III

Literature shows us man as he sees himself, and even when, as in tragic poetry, it shows us the world common to all, adding artistic detachment to insight, this world is still a personal world, with human values at its center.

"The world common to all": at this point we reach the question of the social function of literature. What is the source of our democratic principles? [1] Who supports them? Let us look once more at the antithetical views of man, centering our attention on the ideas of human significance, equality, and freedom.

The first antithesis: the significance of the individual.

As he sees himself, man is the most significant of beings, the center of his universe. He is the ultimate reality; he and his values are the measures of all things.

Viewed and measured externally, however, man is a midge, an ephemeris, a shrinking mite in an expanding universe; his sense of importance in the scheme of things is, like all his opinions and values, a subjective illusion; and his claim that he is too precious to be subordinated to the will and needs of the state lacks supporting evidence.

The second antithesis: the idea of human equality.

Viewed with insight, men are equal in human worth and equal in the sense that all share a common fate. As he sees

[1] For a discussion of this question, see H. A. Myers, *Are Men Equal? An Inquiry into the Meaning of American Democracy* (New York: G. P. Putnam's Sons, 1945; reissued Ithaca, N.Y.: Cornell University Press, 1955).

himself, each individual is supremely important, and since one supremely important individual cannot be more or less important than other supremely important individuals, all are equal in human worth—the true meaning of equality. As human beings, moreover, all are joined together in what Hawthorne once called the kinship of a common fate.

Viewed and measured from the outside, however, men are unequal in every respect: in size, shape, color, strength, wealth, social position, intelligence, and virtue. If the measurements are precise enough, it is unlikely that we shall ever find two individuals who are equal in any single respect: it is inconceivable that two men should be found equal in all measurable respects.

The third antithesis: freedom and responsibility.

As every individual knows, judging by his own feelings, and as literature testifies, man has an inner sense of freedom and responsibility. This sense is the foundation of his moral life since, if he lacked it, praise or blame for his conduct, and satisfaction or remorse on his part, would be equally pointless. This sense is also foundational to free institutions—to religion, law, education, and private enterprise as they exist in a democracy.

Judged impersonally, however, and from the outside, man is not free; his every act is seen, from this point of view, as a link in a chain of cause and effect; at best his every choice is determined by a motive, as Jonathan Edwards pointed out; at worst his conduct is altogether determined by such impersonal and blind forces as heredity and environment.

When we consider these antithetical views of man, we discover at once the source of our democratic principles.

Since the supremacy of the individual, the equality of men in human worth and rights, and the freedom and responsibility of the individual are the axioms of democracy, it is evident that American civilization rests on a foundation of insight and that literature, with insight as its essence, is indispensable to our culture. The insighted writer meets each measurement of the external insignificance of man with an undaunted reaffirmation of man's inner view that he is at the center of things and supremely important. The great writer strengthens our self-respect and helps it to flower into respect for others by deepening our sense of equality; he reminds us that our sense of freedom and responsibility is a "stubborn fact" in our experience and that we cannot escape from our consciences by retreating into the impersonal world of mathematics and measurement.

## IV

The axioms of democracy—the doctrines of the supremacy of the individual, of the equality of men, and of man's freedom and responsibility—are derived from insight, and cannot be verified by external measurements. Unfortunately, those of us who wish to defend these axioms are handicapped by the fact that our culture is out of balance. Its respect for science is one of its glories, but its lack of respect for literature is a grave error of judgment. Why is our culture out of balance? Why do we respect objectivity only and neglect insight? Why do we regard science as a necessity and literature as a luxury?

One reason is that we are in a period of reaction against excessive claims made in the past for poetry and poetic intuition. After Immanuel Kant had apparently shown, late in the eighteenth century, that scientific reason falls into hopeless contradiction when it is applied to such questions as the existence of God and the immortality of the soul, poets were encouraged to answer transcendental questions on intuitive grounds. Wordsworth feels the presence of God in nature and has intuitive intimations of immortality. Whitman tells us again and again that he knows he is immortal. Tennyson speaks with final confidence of

> One God, one law, one element,
> And one far-off divine event,
> To which the whole creation moves.

We respect these convictions as evidences of faith, but we have every reason to believe that the intuitions upon which the nineteenth-century poets and prophets relied cannot be empirically verified. Although literature adequately reveals the hopes and fears and the doubts and beliefs of men concerning things beyond our present experience, literature as such cannot turn faith into certainty. Those who insist, for example, that the Bible is only great literature must look elsewhere for certainty about the supernatural; and those who accept the Bible as divinely inspired are relying on a power far beyond the natural powers of the poet. Few people today would agree with Matthew Arnold, who believed that poetry will replace theology and the poet replace the theologian. T. S. Eliot is much closer to the truth in maintaining that nothing can ever be a satisfactory substitute for something else.

The poetic insight which I have been describing as the essence of literature is altogether different from the intuition of the nineteenth-century prophet. The prophet's intuitions about the transcendental and the supernatural cannot be demonstrated and, without the support of faith, must always remain conjectural; the poet's insights into present experience, however, may be demonstrated and may be tested by further experience and shown to be either true or false.

Most present-day critics and poets, in their reaction against the exaggerated claims made for prophetic intuition, have unfortunately gone to the other extreme. For them poetry is a purely aesthetic experience which has little or nothing to do with either meaning or morality. To go to this extreme is to throw out the baby with the bath water. Although we must reject the prophet's claim that, through intuition, he can offer us assurances about God and the hereafter, we should recognize that the poet, if he is gifted with insight, is a trustworthy observer of the life of man here and now.

A second reason for our failure to understand the nature and function of literature is the old but as yet unexploded notion that there can be only one trustworthy source of knowledge. Poets, philosophers, rhetoricians, theologians, and scientists of many varieties, exact and social, have too often been rivals rather than collaborators in the pursuit of knowledge. Each has at some time or other sought recognition as the only reliable teacher. This rivalry, which arises from the natural tendency of every man to overestimate the worth of what he knows best, or can do best, can be traced from its beginnings in Plato's attack on the poets through the attack on the philosophers by the rhetoricians, Isocrates and Quintilian, and on up to the present time. A wise man, after judiciously weighing the claims of each of the rivals, might well conclude that each has had, and still has, something valuable to contribute. Unfortunately, however, our age still honors the notion that there is only one trustworthy source of knowledge. The present-day form of this notion is a vague but widespread popular faith that statistics and other forms of external measurement will soon place poetry, metaphysics, theology, rhetoric, and ethics in a class with alchemy and astrology. Our age might well be called the Age of the Apotheosis of Objectivity.

The main reason why our culture is out of balance is, of course, that we have failed to understand the true nature and social function of literature. The burden of the problem of restoring the cultural balance falls largely on interpreters of literature, on critics, scholars, and teachers, who should, I believe, devote a little less time to purely aesthetic and technical studies, to the elucidation of puzzling texts, and to literary history, and a little more time to the heart of literature—insight.

Our generation has been so deeply impressed by the great achievements of scientists and technicians that it has forgotten the indispensable contributions of poets and artists. It is the special duty of a professor of literature to remind it that the axioms of democracy are derived from insight and that sympathetic insight, the ability of one man to take another man's point of view, is, and always will be, the only cement which can hold a free society together.

An ideal democratic culture depends upon our realization that the views of man afforded by literature and by science are complementary, not contradictory, and that only by combining these views can we hope to come close to the full truth about ourselves. In a progressive and successful democracy man must be weighed and measured by science as well as esteemed through insight.

As the poets proclaim, man has significance and dignity —that is, he has a value beyond measuring—but, as the scientists point out, he is also a relatively weak and insignificant being, who must measure his strength carefully before judging the feasibility of any enterprise. Man is a free and responsible being, but his freedom and responsibility are limited by heredity, by environment, by capacities and incapacities which we must carefully measure if we are to reward or punish him justly for his actions. All men are equal in human worth and in the kinship of a common fate, but they are unequal in every other respect, and only by careful measuring and testing can we help each individual to find the place in society in which he can do his best.

In these ways, the poet and the scientist, properly understood, are always at work, each contributing his indispensable share to the building of our society and the perfection of our democratic justice. Indeed, the poet and the scientist are not rivals but equal and trustworthy partners in the greatest of all tasks, the task of teaching man through insight to see others as he sees himself and through objectivity to see himself as others see him.

✲✲✲

# Acknowledgments

# and Sources

THE essays and lectures in this volume have been taken from the following sources:

I. From the *International Journal of Ethics* (The University of Chicago Press), April, 1935.

II. From the *Educational Theatre Journal*, December, 1949.

III. From "Captain Ahab's Discovery: The Tragic Meaning of *Moby Dick*," *New England Quarterly*, March, 1942, with additions from "The Tragic Spirit in America," originally given as the second of three public lectures at the University of London, November, 1951.

IV. From the author's notes on Whitman and from "Whitman's Conception of the Spiritual Democracy, 1855–1856" and "Whitman's Consistency," *American Literature* (Duke University Press), November, 1934 and November, 1936.

V. From "Macbeth and the Tragedy of Equivalence," which the author read at the annual Shakespeare Festival at Hofstra College, Hempstead, Long Island, on April 25, 1953.

VI. From "Tragedy and Comedy: *Romeo and Juliet* and A

*Midsummer Night's Dream,"* which was read before the Stanford Philological Association, Stanford University, California, on October 22, 1953.

VII. From *Essays in Political Theory, Presented to George H. Sabine* (Ithaca, N.Y.: Cornell University Press, 1948).

VIII. From three public lectures given at the University of London in November, 1951: (1) "Change of Fortune: The Nature of Tragedy," (2) "The Tragic Spirit in America," and (3) "Tragedy and Modern Times."

IX. From "Dramatic Poetry and Values," *English Journal,* May, 1939, with later revisions and with additions from "Scholasticism in Modern Thought," *Journal of Philosophy,* March, 1939.

X. From the *Pacific Spectator* (Stanford University Press), Autumn, 1954.

The publishers of the periodicals listed above have kindly granted permission for the articles originally published by them to be reprinted.

✢✢✢

# Index

*205*

# Index

# Index

Marlowe, Christopher, 7, 10, 70, 137, 159, 181

*Master Builder, The,* 7, 10, 15, 160

Mathematics, 3, 177, 181, 183, 198

Matthiessen, F. O., 101-102, 167-168

*Medea,* 157-158

Melodrama, 40-42, 60, 106, 155-157, 159, 165

Melville, Herman, 57-78, 137; see also *Moby Dick*

Meredith, George, 144

*Metabasis, see* Change of fortune

*Midsummer Night's Dream, A,* 110-128

Milton, John, 10, 19, 23, 192

*Moby Dick,* 45, 57-77, 137, 157, 159, 188, 192, 194-195; allegory in, 61-63; discovery in, 59, 64, 66, 71-72, 74-75; dramatic form of, 66-67; reversal in, 66; symbolism in, 61, 67, 72-73; tragic hero in, 64, 68-71

Moderation, 131-137, 147-148, 158

*Mourning Becomes Electra,* 22-23

*Murder in the Cathedral,* 192

Necessary sequence of events, 34, 36, 49, 170, 183

Newton, Sir Isaac, 180, 190

*Nichomachean Ethics,* 41-46, 135-136

Nietzsche, F. W., 134-136, 143, 145, 170

*November Boughs,* 79

Objectivity, 65, 127-128, 177-179, 194-196, 198, 201-202

*Oedipus at Colonus,* 35, 37

*Oedipus the King,* 14, 17, 35-38, 66, 139, 154, 157, 163, 181, 188

*Omoo,* 65

O'Neill, Eugene, 10, 22-23, 36; ambivalence in, 99-102; tragic insight of, 160

Optimism, 5, 12, 75-76, 88-89, 102, 156, 166, 168

Orderliness: of nature, 182; in tragedy, 127-128; of values, 4, 11, 21-22

*Oresteia,* 22-23, 26, 157-158, 190

*Othello,* 15, 26, 105, 139, 154, 157, 159, 181, 194-195

*Paradise Lost,* 192

Peabody, J. P., 99

*Peer Gynt,* 142

Personal perspective, theory of, 178

Pessimism, 5, 12, 88, 156, 170

*Philebus,* 112

Philosophy of values, 3-4, 21-22, 25-27

*Pierre,* 77

Plato, 23, 27, 30-31, 110-113, 146, 200

Plot, 18-20, 33-41, 52-53, 65-67

Poe, E. A., 78, 81, 192

Poetic justice, *see* Justice, poetic

*Poetics,* 28-53, 134-135, 190

*Politics,* 50-51

Problem play, 41

Progress, 166-168

# Index